Companions in Commerce

Discover the Untold Sahabah Stories of Inspiring Businesswomen in Early Islam

SARAH GULFRAZ

Dedication

~ Bismillah ~

May Allah (swt) accept our efforts and grant us success in this life and
the next. Ameen.

In dedication to my loving family and all their support.

Contents

1. Introduction to the Businesswomen of Early Islam   1
   The Role of Women in Pre-Islamic Arabia
   The Influence of Women in Early Islam

2. Khadijah Bint Khuwaylid: First and Foremost   16
   Early Life and Background
   Her Partnership with the Holy Prophet
   The Business Empire
   Services to Islam

3. Umm Salamah: Wisdom and Wealth   36
   From Wealth to Widowhood
   Her Business Activities
   Contributions to Islamic Knowledge
   Role in Islamic Jurisprudence

4. Asma Bint Abu Bakr: The Resourceful Trader   50
   Early Life and Family Influence
   Her Initial Challenges
   Hazrat Asma (RA) Qualities
   Entrepreneurial Spirit

5. Zaynab Bint Jahsh: Leatherwork to Leadership   60
   Early Life and Family Background
   Marriage to the Prophet Muhammad
   Lessons to be Learned from Her Life
   Her Leatherwork Business

6. Fatimah bint Muhammad: A Life of Devotion   73
   The Beloved Daughter

A Life of Virtue and Wisdom
Her Knowledge and Wisdom
Hazrat Fatima (RA) as a Role Model

7. Umm Sharik and Umm Ruman: Unsung Heroines 90
Steadfastness of Hazrat Umm Sharik (RA)
The Patience of Umm Ruman (RA)

8. Conclusion: Lessons from the Past 97
Importance of Female Entrepreneurs in Islam
Inspiring Future Generations
Creating Balance is Mandatory
Continuing the Legacy

Find Out More 107

Introduction to the Businesswomen of Early Islam

Women are considered the backbone of any country. Early Islam played a significant role in women's lives. In addition to being moms, wives, and daughters, they were businesswomen, leaders, and academics deeply engaged in every facet of society, from politics and religion to business and economics.

Islam has long viewed business as a vital means of subsistence. As a result, it has a unique entrepreneurial culture with tenets drawn from the Quran and the Sunnah. Under Islamic law, women are not prohibited from working or running businesses.

Rather, Islamic law entitles a Muslim woman to own property, earn money from business and other professional endeavours, enter into contracts, and handle all of her assets as she sees fit. She is free to manage her own company, and no one, not even her spouse, can deduct her earnings as long as she upholds Islamic norms of decency and morality. Numerous Muslim women have excelled in the domains of education, business, and medicine throughout Islamic history. Even in the Prophet's (PBUH) day, women traded, and the Prophet encouraged women to enter the economic world. Women are granted numerous rights and obligations and have elevated status according to the Quran and Hadith.

> *In the Quran, Allah says: "And for women are a share of what they have earned, and for men is a share of what they have earned. And ask Allah of His bounty. Indeed, Allah is ever, of all things, knowing." (Quran 4: 32)*

According to the Quran, women and men are equal in terms of humanity and spirituality. It also allows women to inherit money, own property, and run their own businesses. The rights of women were championed by the Prophet Muhammad (PBUH).

He (PBUH) encouraged women to pursue education and become involved in society. Additionally, he appointed women to top roles. Islam accords women a high standing, as seen by the role played by women in its early chapters. Islam encourages women to fully engage in all facets of society, acknowledging their unique talents and contributions.

The Role of Women in Pre-Islamic Arabia

Women's status varied greatly in pre-Islamic Arabia based on the rules and customs of the tribes where they resided. Therefore, before the arrival of Islam, there was no clear description of the roles that women played and the rights that they enjoyed.

Prior to Islam, most countries regarded women as inferior and base. They used to think that she was the origin of evil and sin, that she was formed from a low soul, and that she was not a human creature with a soul. Fourteen centuries ago, in human history, a precedent was created by the recognition that Islam bestowed upon women.

For Arab women, Islam was a liberating force that lifted them out of the possession and accessory position of pre-Islamic society. In its first legal codes, Islam acknowledged women as autonomous entities with rights and obligations.

Arab civilisation prior to Islam was typified by social and ethnic ties to powerful patriarchal institutions. In this pre-Islamic era, women were stripped of most of their civic rights and advantages during the pre-Islamic era because society did not value their uniqueness. They did not inherit anything or have any privileges, being viewed as rubbish or pieces of property.

A prevalent practice of the burying of daughters alive, driven by the belief that doing so would erase any associated shame. Consequently, many parents preferred not to have daughters, as having a girl was considered a great shame to the family, particularly for those considered to be nobles, wealthy, or other influential members of the community.

A man would typically keep the news closely guarded so that no one else would learn that their wife had given birth to a daughter. Out of shame, they would not even think twice about killing the baby girl. The alternative was to keep the child, although this was done in a way devoid of justice or humanity.

One particularly abhorrent story tells of a father who was travelling abroad when his wife gave birth. When he returned, he snatched his daughter from her mother, dug a hole while she was cleaning the dust off his clothes, and then, without warning, shoved the girl into the hole and covered her with dust as she cried out in sympathy. However, he remained unmoved by her.

The Quran describes this circumstance when Allah (SWT) says:

"And when the girl [who was] buried alive is asked for what sin she was killed." (Quran 81:8-9)

Due to their strong distaste for girls, some men would openly display sadness upon learning that their wives had given birth to a girl. They would then debate whether to bury the girl alive or subject her to the shame of living. Allah the Almighty says:

> *"And when one of them is informed of [the birth of] a female, his face becomes dark, and he suppresses grief. He hides himself from the people because of the ill of which he has been informed. Should he keep it in humiliation or bury it in the ground? Unquestionably, evil is what they decide." (Quran 16:58-59)*

This terrible fate terrified some mothers. During pregnancy, a mother might dig a hole herself, planning to throw her newborn daughter into it if she gave birth, protecting her from the catastrophe that would occur when the father returned. After giving birth, some mothers would strangle their newborn daughters.

If a girl survived, she was compelled to get married at the tender age of seven or eight years old. The practice of child marriage arose from parents' fear that their daughters would be defiled if not married before reaching adolescence.

During this time, Arabs married by purchase, contact, and imprisonment. There were no laws or regulations dictating how many wives an Arab might have. A woman was, therefore, viewed as a type of property. Women could be presented to guests as a sign of hospitality. Although there was no joint right for women in the pre-Islamic era, husbands were allowed to divorce their wives anytime they felt like it.

Two things motivated their dislike of girls: first, girls did not fight in battles. Second, there was a fear that a girl might someday cause them embarrassment. Oddly enough, despite their embarrassment over daughters, many Arab tribes were somewhat tolerant of prostitution. Until Allah (SWT) revealed the verse prohibiting it, they even compelled their slave females into prostitution:

> *"And do not compel your slave girls to prostitution, if they desire chastity, to seek [thereby] the temporary interests of worldly life. And if someone should compel them, then indeed, Allah is [to them], after their compulsion, Forgiving and Merciful." (Quran 24:33)*

Let us examine more closely the ways that pre-Islamic and Islamic Arabic women's lives differed in relation to the following institutions:

Social Status and Restrictions

According to Goetheater, the man was the family's owner and had the right to live with women and children during the pre-Islamic era. During this time of ignorance, the woman was viewed as a second-class human being and was not seen as a member of the human race.

In pre-Islamic Arabia, women's treatment and social standing varied greatly, primarily according to the tribe and area in which they resided. Although a few women managed to achieve positions of authority and dignity in their societies, the majority faced discriminatory and patriarchal practices and were perceived as less valuable than men.

Before Islam arrived, women in Arabia were often not given any legal position under the customary tribal law that predated Islam. The tribe, comprised of individuals with ties to a common relative, served as the primary functional unit of Arabian society.

In these patriarchal tribes, property could only be inherited by males; women were not allowed to inherit. The spoken norms of the tribe, which mostly restricted women's rights, were upheld by the tribal chief. Women were frequently viewed as property that might be inherited or taken during a tribal war.

In some tribes, for example, the notion that male babies were more valued than female ones led to a widespread practice of female infanticide. In addition, women were not allowed to inherit property, and their evidence was frequently ignored in court. Other prevalent practices were forced marriages, restricted rights for divorce and child custody, and early marriages to much older men.

Matrimony was not only a matter of personal preference in pre-Islamic Arabia's intricate and demanding society but also an essential tool for creating and preserving social order and tribal identity. Unfortunately, women were frequently caught amid these alliances and disputes, with males and tribe politics deciding on their lives and prospects.

Even a cursory look at Arabia's history before the arrival of Islam would reveal that women were considered a liability to a tribe in pre-Islamic Arabia because they lacked certain qualities that were essential to a nomadic society, such as the ability to fight, attack animals, and seize food. In addition, women were weakened by pregnancy or bound by childrearing for a large portion of their lives.

Thus, societal conditions and the need for survival influenced women's low status in that community. Another aspect contributing to women's poor standing was that older male family members kept their daughters within the house, restricting their involvement in society to protect their virginal reputation and quality and, consequently, the honour of their family members.

Moreover, the poor position of women in that society was partly caused by men's unrestricted right to polygamy, which was based only on a man's capacity to seduce or buy women. Put simply, women did not have the right to leave a man. She was not entitled to inherit. She was completely reliant on the men in her community and was vulnerable.

Before the advent of Islam, women in pre-Islamic Arabia lived under a system that denied them basic rights and dignity. According to the Quran, during the pre-Islamic era known as Jahiliyyah (period of ignorance), Arab women used to bury their daughters alive. There were two reasons for this fear: first, that having more females would burden the economy; second, they feared the shame that sometimes followed when girls were taken prisoner by an enemy tribe and later showed preference for their captors over their brothers and parents.

Economic Participation

Prior to Islam, women everywhere, even in pre-Islamic Arabia, were forced into service and enslavement. They were even viewed as a financial burden. During that time, one of the biggest economic disadvantages women faced was being unable to inherit. Generally speaking, women had no inheritance rights. Instead, they were the inheritable portion of a husband's fortune.

Except in the affluent classes and large urban centres, women who relied on men for survival had no property rights. In the past, women had little political or decision-making power in day-to-day tribal affairs; instead, the tribal chief made all of the choices on behalf of the tribe.

Women had no notion of their own existence or identity, with men having absolute control over their rights, freedoms, and dignity. Men could regulate every aspect of women's lives —personal, social, or professional—according to their wishes. Therefore, in these conservative countries, the concept of women's rights was either nonexistent or extremely limited, and the phrase "socio-economic empowerment of women" was unheard of.

Transformation with the Advent of Islam

Before the advent of Islam, women were oppressed and forced to endure excessive suffering throughout human history. Throughout all previous civilisations, they suffered from intolerable poverty, misery, and subjugation. Stated differently, they were handled as though they were not human.

Following a protracted period of injustice, Allah, the Most Exalted, bestowed humanity with mercy via the teachings of Islam, whose teachings changed the dark history of humanity and brought about a way of life that no human civilisation had ever experienced before for Arab women,

Islam was a liberating force that lifted them out of the possession and accessory position of pre-Islamic society. In its first legal codes, Islam acknowledged women as autonomous entities with rights and obligations.

With the arrival of Islam, the emphasis switched from the tribe to the individual, balanced by the ideas of family and community. This resulted in the establishment of an egalitarian society where people of all genders, races, ages, and socioeconomic status were treated equally. Women's rights in Islam were determined by moral and religious precepts rather than tribal affinities.

Islam recognised women as independent human beings with complete legal rights. Female infanticide was one of the cruel and oppressive practices against women that Islam rectified or outlawed. Islam restored women's rights wherever they had been violated or disregarded.

Islam views women as a particular blessing, with the same rights and obligations as men. Women are of the greatest importance, as the holy book of the Quran and the early history of Islam attests to. Islam accorded women dignity and unparalleled protection. To understand how Islam empowers women, consider this summary of women's rights: Islam made a woman an heir, even in an era when women were seen as property to be inherited.

Depending on their relationship to the deceased relative and the total number of heirs, daughters, wives, mothers, and sisters all receive a different portion of the inheritance. A lady cannot be relieved of her inherited portion of the property by anybody.

Additionally, women have no financial obligations. They are not required to share household expenses or work. With her own money, whether it comes from her father or something she works for herself, a woman has the right to work or support herself as long as her integrity and honour are maintained.

There is no shortage of evidence to support the claim that Islam is the true religion that frees women from enslavement. To make this clearer, we'll explain how Islam defends a woman's rights from the moment she is a foetus in her mother's womb until she dies and meets her Lord. Let's investigate!

Regarding a person's relationship to Allah, there is no distinction made in Islam between men and women because both are assured of receiving the same reward for good deeds and punishment for bad deeds.

Allah says in the Quran: "And for women are rights over men similar to those of men over women." (Quran 2:226)

Women have actively participated in society's operations since the dawn of Islam. Islam is replete with instances of women holding significant positions. Some even served as nurses tending to the injured or appeared on the front lines.

Prophet Muhammad's (PBUH) first wife, Hazrat Khadijah (RA), was a formidable force in the trading world. Islam permits women to have any kind of leadership or governmental position and does not view them as inferior to men. One of the few women who could read and write at the time, Al-Shifa bint Abdullah was chosen by Hazrat Umer, the second Caliph, to be the marketplace supervisor.

"Hazrat Umm Salamah used to lead women in prayer and stood in the middle." (Al-Bayhaqi)

The Quran uses the most exquisite simile to highlight the fundamental unity of men and women:

> *"They (your wives) are your garment, and you are a garment for them." (Quran 2:187)*

Husband and wife secure each other's virginity by entering into a marriage, much as a robe conceals our nudity. The clothing provides comfort to the body, and the husband and wife both enjoy comfort in each other's companionship. Just as clothing embodies elegance, beauty, and decoration, so too do wives represent their husbands to them in return.

Moreover, according to Hazrat Muhammad (PBUH), education is a must for all Muslims, regardless of gender. The Holy Prophet's (PBUH) wife, Aisha (R.A), was regarded as one of the most important academics in Islamic history.

> *The Holy Prophet said: "Procurement of knowledge is essential for all Muslims [both men and women with no discernment]." (Ibn Majah)*

Islam upholds the rights of women as they existed before birth, when Allah (SWT) bestowed upon them the right to rule alongside males on earth and created Hawwa' (Eve), may Allah glorify her name, to share religious duties with Adam.

> *Allah Almighty Says: "And [mention, O Muhammad], when your Lord said to the angels, "Indeed, I will make upon the earth a successive authority." (Quran 2:30)*

Islam has protected women's rights and gender equality in all areas of their lives. Islam forbids discrimination against men and women and guarantees the equal rights of men and women. Let's have a closer look at some specific orders of Allah Almighty in the light of the Holy Quran:

Islam called women a gift to humanity, defending their rights. Allah says in the Quran:

"He gives to whom He wills female [children], and He gives to whom He wills males." (Quran 42:49)

Islam generally safeguards a woman's inheritance rights, regardless of age.

Allah says: "But if there are [only] daughters, two or more, for them is two-thirds of one's estate. And if there is only one, for her is half." (Quran 4:11)

Islam safeguards her status in society by holding her accountable for the emergence of virtue and the eradication of vice by encouraging what is good and prohibiting what is evil, much like man. She was created in this manner to bear the weight of religious duty and the summons to Allah as a trust for which both she and man would answer to the Almighty Allah.

"The believing men and believing women are allies of one another. They enjoin what is right and forbid what is wrong and establish prayer and give Zakah [obligatory charity] and obey Allah and His Messenger. Those - Allah will have mercy upon them. Indeed, Allah is exalted in Might and Wise." (Quran 9:71)

Islam upholds women's rights by forbidding the practice of burying them alive and by making it mandatory to give them a decent upbringing and education.

Allah says, "And when the girl [who was] buried alive is asked - for what sin she was killed." (Quran 81:8-9)

The Prophet Muhammad's teachings and actions have significant implications for women's rights in Islam. Here are some key points based on the Prophet Muhammad's teachings and practices regarding women:

The Messenger of Allah (PBUH) said: "Whoever has a female child whom he neither buries alive, nor humiliates, and never favours a male child of his over her, Allah will admit him to Paradise." (Sunan Abi Dawud)

Islam even forbids polytheistic women from dying in battle, thereby defending their lives. According to Ibn Umar, may Allah be pleased with him, it was related that he said,

"A woman was found killed during one of the battles led by the Prophet (PBUH) thereupon he (PBUH) forbade killing women and children (in wars)." (Al-Bukhari, Muslim)

Islam upholds women's rights by placing Paradise—the ultimate goal for all believers—beneath her feet. How wonderful the woman's Islamic honour is! The Prophet Muhammad (PBUH) stated:

*"(The way to) Paradise lies beneath the feet of mothers
."(Sunan an-Nasai)*

Islam grants women all of their civic rights, hence protecting their rights. As a result, she gained the authority to sign agreements for the sale, purchase, partnership, loan, mortgage, gift, and other purposes. Islam upholds women's rights by removing the perpetual status of minorhood from them, recognising their full legal capacity and granting them guardianship over their belongings and other matters.

Islam not only protected women but also established rights for them at a time when the rest of the world ignored them. In light of this, it's absurd for anyone to believe that women in Islam are less valuable than men. Each contributes uniquely to maintaining the harmony of society as a whole. Nonetheless, Islam raised women's standing to parity with males and restored their dignity.

The Influence of Women in Early Islam

Contributions to Islamic Society

Early Islam played a pivotal role for women, who actively participated in every facet of society, including politics, religion, the arts, and the economy. Islam accords women a high standing, as seen by the role played by women in its early chapters.

Islam encourages women to fully engage in all facets of society, acknowledging their special talents and contributions. More than 1400 years ago, our Prophet (PBUH) taught the world the inherent worth of women. Through Islam, he empowered women, inspiring them to reach their full potential as virtuous slaves of Allah (SWT). The Prophet Muhammad (PBUH) championed women's rights, advocating for their education, involvement in society, and placement in positions of authority.

In contrast to prevailing social norms, Muslim women played significant roles throughout the lifetime of the Prophet Muhammad (PBUH). His spouse, Aisha (RA), was a learned woman who freely asserted herself in public and was once sought out for advice on religious matters by other associates. She went so far as to commend the Ansar women for overcoming their shyness to inquire about Islam and become knowledgeable about their faith.

Aisha (RA) taught the companions after the Prophet Muhammad (PBUH) passed away. She was one of the most learned people of the period since she was the closest person to the Prophet (PBUH). Many of the hadiths she continued passing on to those around her were inherited from the Prophet (PBUH). She became a vital source of inspiration for Islamic tradition and was instrumental in spreading the teachings of the Prophet (PBUH). Among the things she left behind for the next generation was her contributions to Islamic studies.

Other examples of the role of women in early Islam

Leaders: In the early days of Islam, women occupied leadership roles as well. As previously established, Aisha bint Abu Bakr (RA) served as a prominent advisor to both Abu Bakr (RA) and Hazrat Umar (RA), the caliphs. In the Battle of the Camel, she led her own army and was a well-known military figure.

Teachers and scholars: Women were instrumental in the transmission and preservation of Islamic knowledge. They were experts and instructors in law, theology, philosophy, and other Islamic sciences in addition to the Quran and Hadith. Among the most well-known female intellectuals in early Islam were Hazrat Fatima bint al-Mundhir, Hazrat Umm Salamah (RA), and Hazrat Aisha bint Abu Bakr (RA).

Businesswomen: Early Islam's economy included women as well. They engaged in trade and commerce in addition to owning and running their own companies. For instance, the Prophet Muhammad's (PBUH) first wife, Hazrat Khadijah (RA), was a prosperous businesswoman. Islam tells us that women have numerous rights and obligations and that they are just as human and spiritual as men.

Islam made women the reason fathers would reach paradise, placing paradise at their feet when they became mothers. They also made wives so essential to a husband's faith that his faith would remain incomplete without honouring her. With this newfound power, women rose to prominence and left their stamp on history, ensuring they would not be forgotten when the greats of Islam were exalted.

Islam changed women's status overnight by acting as a catalyst in their lives and as a source of direction for all of humanity. Women's rights, a notion that had never been heard of or even considered, were being defended and safeguarded. Wives evolved from being only a domestic commodity to a source of dignity. As a result, Muslim women served as intellectuals, jurists, benefactresses, monarchs, businesswomen, warriors, and legal experts who contributed to the heritage of Islam.

This book aims to provide a comprehensive understanding of the influential businesswomen in early Islam, highlighting their significant contributions and lasting legacies. Beginning with an exploration of the role of women in pre-Islamic Arabia and their subsequent influence in early Islam, the book sets the stage for detailed profiles of notable figures.

Chapter Two

Khadijah Bint Khuwaylid: First and Foremost

Muslim women have been pioneers in entrepreneurship, shattering stereotypes and opening doors for later generations. These ladies have left a significant legacy that motivates and empowers women everywhere. In addition to affecting their local communities, their contributions to philanthropy, invention, and education have also impacted the world economy.

It's a common misconception in today's world—one marred by societal prejudices—that Islam is to blame for Muslim women's subjugation and lack of independence. But inspirational ladies like Hazrat Khadijah (RA) have demonstrated throughout their lives that such assertions are untrue.

The fact that Hazrat Khadijah (RA) was an educated, prosperous businesswoman, her family's only provider, and, at one point, a working single mother is sufficient evidence against the assertion that Islam oppresses women. The 7th-century woman Khadijah bint Khuwaylid (RA) is regarded as the first Muslim woman entrepreneur. She was a wonderful person.

Early Life and Background

Noble Lineage and Upbringing

Hazrat Khadijah (RA) is descended from a great Quraish family. She was born in 565 AD to Khuwailid and Fatima (RA). Her father was a prominent Makkah leader known for his prosperous trade in exotic goods such as oils, linen, perfumes, and more. Fatima's mother was the daughter of Zaida ibn al-Asam of Banu (Amir ibn Luayy ibn Ghalib) and a distant relative of the Prophet Muhammad (PBUH). The family resided close to the Kabah in a two-story home next to a hill.

Hazrat Khadijah (RA) obtained two titles: Ameerat Quraish, Princess of Quraish, as well as Tahira, the Pure One, because of her flawless personality and noble character, not to mention her honourable descent, despite the horribly male-chauvinistic environment in which she was born.

The Makkah community bestowed upon her the term *Taahirah*, which translates to "the Pure" or "Virtuous," in recognition of her moral merits. She had a kind and sympathetic heart. Hazrat Khadijah (RA) exhibited good traits from an early age and developed into a peaceful, thoughtful, and devout young woman.

She was known for her generosity towards her relatives. She provided them with financial assistance, food, and clothes and even arranged for the marriage of her kin, who would not have otherwise been able to marry. She was exceedingly charitable with her wealth.

It is said that after Muhammad (PBUH) married Hazrat Khadijah (RA), Haleemah (RA) of the Banu Sa'd tribe—the woman who had cared for him as a child—once visited him. Muhammad (PBUH) had lived with the Banu Sa'd clan for five years, and he carried a grateful memory of the kindness he had received from them as a young child. As a result, when Haleemah (RA) arrived, he treated her with enormous respect and had previously spoken highly of her to Hazrat Khadijah (RA).

Hazrat Khadijah (RA) was also delighted to see her. It was a dry year, and the lack of water killed trees, crops, and wild flora. Many animals perished from starvation, reducing them to skeletons.

People in the nation were concerned about the food shortage. Haleemah (RA) spent some time living with the Holy Prophet's (PBUH) family. When she decided to return to her parents, she received forty sheep and a she-camel from Hazrat Khadijah (RA). Haleemah (RA) and her family were incredibly appreciative of that kindness.

Introduction to Trade and Business

Following Khuwayled's father's death, Hazrat Khadijah (RA) assumed leadership of the family enterprise and expeditiously grew it. With the money she made, she assisted the underprivileged, widows, orphans, the ill, and the disabled. Hazrat Khadijah (RA) married off any impoverished girls and provided them with a dowry.

She received business advice from one of her uncles, and when she asked for help, other family members also helped her with business management. However, she made her own decisions and did not rely on anyone else. Though she appreciated and took into consideration recommendations, she trusted her own judgement. One thing the elders in her family knew she disliked was paternalism.

Travelling with the caravans allowed the majority of businessmen who had goods to sell in Yemen or Syria to supervise every transaction personally. However, in times when a trader found himself stuck in Makkah, he hired a man to accompany the caravan in his place. The individual selected for this role needed to have a solid reputation for integrity and great business judgement, commonly referred to as a manager or agent.

Hazrat Khadijah (RA) was a homebody and did not want to go with the caravans, nor did she have brothers and relatives. As a result, whenever a caravan was prepared to travel overseas, she hired an agent and gave him the task of transporting and selling her merchandise there.

She eventually became the wealthiest trader in Makkah thanks to her astute agent selection, timing, and strategic buying and selling. She also made enormous profits. According to Ibn Sa'ad's Tabaqat, Hazrat Khadijah's (RA) cargo alone was worth the combined cargo of all the Quraish merchants whenever caravans of Makkah merchants set off on their voyage.

Everyone could see that she possessed the elusive "golden touch." She could turn dust into gold by touching it. The people of Makkah gave her the title of "the Princess of the Quraish" and also referred to her as "the Makkah Princess." She was the richest lady in Arabia, a trader and a prosperous businesswoman who gained respect from Makkah's business community and was known as "Al-Kubra" (literally, "the Great").

Furthermore, Hazrat Khadijah (RA) was the only woman to receive a greeting from Allah Almighty through the Angel Jibril (AS). Jibril (AS) then sent this information to the Prophet (PBUH), who was overjoyed to hear that his wife would enter Paradise.

> *Hazrat Ali (RA) said: "I heard Holy Prophet (PBUH) saying: "The best woman (of the world in his time) was Maryam, the daughter of 'Imran, and the best woman (of this community) is Khadijah (bint Khuwaylid)"(Al-Bukhari)*

Trading is a talent that Hazrat Khadijah's (RA) father taught her. After his death, her father left his trade firm to his daughter. Hazrat Khadijah (RA) hired men who were dependable, honest, and strong enough to withstand the perilous, lengthy voyages that her commerce caravans would have to make to conduct trade in Yemen, Makkah, and Syria.

Hazrat Khadijah's (RA) skill in selecting profitable partners for all her dealings indicates her ability to assemble a strong team. Put differently, she possessed a highly developed emotional intelligence, also called good intuition.

Moreover, Hazrat Khadijah (RA) inherited her profession and became an entrepreneur thanks to her husband, Abu Hala, a highly successful businessman. She gave him all the support he needed to succeed in the company, but he passed away a few years later.

Through a sequence of events, including the legacy of riches from her father and two husbands, Hazrat Khadijah (RA) became knowledgeable about wealth management strategies and developed the potential to manage her resources prudently and autonomously.

Hazrat Khadijah (RA), who inherited a large fortune and numerous commercial banking establishments, focused on growing her business. She occasionally gave money as a profit to reputable "Quraish" merchants.

Through the simultaneous experience, she was able to advance her career by appointing multiple individuals who were related to her slaves to manage the business operations on her behalf, based on the principles of Ijara, Qirad, and Mudarabah, as per the agreement established. They used to travel to many nations, like Rome, Damascus, Persia, and others, to attend both internal and international markets. These individuals include the Prophet Muhammad (PBUH), Maysarah, Adiyy bn Samit, and others who imported and exported goods like beautiful fabrics sand perfumes. Ultimately, her business continued until her passing.

Her company was the most renowned, with a reputation for honest business practices and superior products. It was bigger than all of the Quraish trades combined. She was undoubtedly a powerful and capable woman in her own right.

To flourish in the male-dominated trades, Hazrat Khadijah (RA) never compromised her integrity or modesty since she knew what she was doing in terms of business. Due to her cunning and commercial acumen, her company became one of the most well-known among the Quraish. She focused all her efforts on growing the company her father had left her.

Since a lot depended on the integrity of the staff members who travelled great distances on her behalf, her policy was to hire diligent, honourable, and distinguished managers to handle matters on her behalf. Her managers purchased things from her exports to resell domestically and shipped them to marketplaces in far-off places. Hence renowned for her extraordinary life, Hazrat Khadijah bint Khuwaylid (RA) is considered the first Muslim woman businesswoman of the seventh century.

Her Earlier Marriages

As Hazrat Khadijah (RA) grew older, her father offered her to Abu Haallah, son of Zaraarah, as a bride. Abu Haallah worked as a trader. Together, they lived a contented life and were blessed with a daughter, Zainab, and a boy, Hind. After a few years, Abu Haallah became unwell and passed away. According to certain historians, Haallah, Hind, and Haarith are the names of Abu Haallah's three sons.

Hazrat Khadijah (RA) wept bitterly over her husband's passing. Afterwards, her father made the wealthy trader 'Ateeq, son of 'Aaiz, his spouse. They were content with their lives until 'Ateeq died returning from a business trip to Syria. From this marriage, she produced one son and a daughter. For the second time, Hazrat Khadijah (RA) became a widow. She turned down marriage proposals from a number of well-known and powerful Quraish men after the passing of her second husband.

She made the decision to live alone and vowed never to get married again. It so happened that her father died not long after her second husband. Hazrat Khadijah (RA), who had to handle the business personally, was greatly saddened by this.

Her Partnership with the Holy Prophet

In 595 AD, she sought someone to manage her caravan to Syria. Hazrat Abu Talib suggested the Prophet Muhammad (PBUH) to her. She had heard of his trustworthiness and integrity and agreed to employ him, although he did not have much trading experience. To help him, she sent her slave Maysara.

She sent him a job offer to head her trading caravans. He gladly accepted the offer and started working for her.

Given the circumstances of her era, it was astonishing that she was well-known in commerce. As a result, she became a marketing genius. Hazrat Khadijah's (RA) significance in Islamic history was further enhanced by her marriage to and subsequent collaboration with the Prophet Muhammad (PBUH).

Her upbringing took place in a setting steeped in commercial culture. Her trading caravans grew to nearly equal the size of all Quraish caravans throughout time. She was trying to find a trading partner she could rely on to deliver her goods. This was the occasion of her meeting with the Prophet Muhammad (PBUH).

Like the rest of his clan, the Prophet Muhammad (PBUH) was a Quraish and depended on trade for his livelihood. He managed the capital of numerous wealthy orphans who couldn't manage their own capital but desired to collaborate with honourable people despite lacking the resources to trade on his own. As a result, the Prophet Muhammad had numerous chances to enter the business world in exchange for a set salary or by sharing profits.

But as mentioned, long before she met the Prophet (PBUH), Hazrat Khadijah (RA) was a prosperous businesswoman. Hazrat Khadijah (RA) discovered the admirable qualities of the Prophet (PBUH) and wanted a specific person to transport her caravan. Every Makkah knew the qualities and gifts that Muhammad (PBUH) possessed from his early years. He had a reputation for being trustworthy, sincere, morally upright, giving, selfless, and helpful. As a result, he was treated with affection and respect. In their era, it was extremely hard to find someone with these qualities.

Muhammad (PBUH) and Hazrat Khadijah (RA) entered into a *Mudarabah* collaboration. Mudarabah literally translates as "to travel for trade, to do business together." According to Islamic law, this kind of partnership is one in which one side provides capital and the other one provides labour. The distribution of the partnership's earnings is based on the partnership ratio that will be decided upon between them.

Before his trip to Syria, Muhammad (PBUH) traded with Hazrat Khadijah (RA). Hazrat Khadijah (RA) grew increasingly confident in the Prophet (PBUH), and at last, she put him in charge of overseeing a caravan that was organised with a sizable and autonomous capital to be sent to Syria.

While Hazrat Khadijah (RA) was searching for a trustworthy person to lead her caravan, Muhammad (PBUH) was working under his uncle, Abu Talib.She approached Muhammad (PBUH) and promised to give him twice as much from the trade's revenues as he paid to other merchants.

Muhammad (PBUH) agreed and was accompanied on the business trip by Hazrat Khadijah's (RA) obedient and seasoned slave Maysarah. Maysarah was struck by the Prophet's honesty, fortitude, devotion to morality, cordial interactions, and commercial acumen.

On his way from Syria, the Prophet (PBUH) stopped to rest under a tree when Nestora, a Jewish monk renowned for his wisdom and religious understanding, spotted him and asked Maysarah who he was. Maysarah filled him in on Muhammad's (PBUH) reputation for integrity and wisdom. Nestora informed him that since only prophets had ever slept beneath that specific tree, this man would eventually be promoted to the prophet status. According to legend, Maysarah also witnessed two angels covering the Prophet's head with a cloud to shield him from the sun's heat and glare.

Upon his return home, Maysarah apprised Hazrat Khadijah (RA) of everything that transpired during the voyage to Syria. She was so pleased and moved that she began considering asking Muhammad (PBUH) to marry her. His noble nature struck Hazrat Khadijah (RA), and she ultimately decided to propose to him. For Hazrat Khadijah (RA), it made no difference how old they were or how different their economic situations were.

But how could she tell him what was on her mind? She has already turned down multiple marriage proposals from men from some of the Quraish's most illustrious families. What would her tribe think? How would her relatives respond? Moreover, would this youthful, single Quraishite warrior accept her offer?

One night, as she wrestled with these issues, she had a vivid dream: she saw the sun descending from the sky and illuminating her house until its rays reached her courtyard. When she awoke, she hurried to her cousin Waraqah bin Nawfal, a blind man renowned for his depth of knowledge, especially on the Torah and the Injil. She sought his interpretation of this remarkable dream.

Upon hearing about her dream, he smiled calmly and assured her that it was a very positive dream. The radiant sun that descended into her courtyard signified the arrival of the Prophet (PBUH), whose coming was prophesied in the Torah and the Injil, and she would benefit from having him in her life.

Then, she approached the Prophet (PBUH) and asked if he would be willing to marry a beautiful lady from a noble and wealthy family inclined to marry him. He asked whom she was referring to; when he learnt her identity, he said that he was willing, provided she was willing to marry him. Hazrat Khadijah (RA) was overjoyed.

She was more determined than ever to wed Muhammad (PBUH) after this encounter with Waraqah. Knowing of her propensity, one of her closest friends, Nafisah bint Manbah, went to Muhammad (PBUH) and asked for permission to ask him a very sensitive question. She questioned why he had not gotten married yet when he replied he had no objections. He claimed he lacked the necessary funds.

After marrying the Prophet (PBUH), Hazrat Khadijah (RA) gave away everything she owned to the poor. After growing up in luxury at her father's affluent home, Hazrat Khadijah (RA) now bravely and patiently endured the financial difficulties that come with any siege. Allah was so delighted with Hazrat Khadijah's (RA) noble demeanour and character that He gave her special greetings. Hazrat Khadijah (RA) was a perfect mother and wife.

The Prophet (PBUH) resided at her home, which was blessed by his presence and the frequent visits from Jibril (AS), who brought him revelations from the Quran. This home soon became a centre for both male and female companions to gather, enjoying the hospitality of Muhammad (PBUH) and his wife, and it eventually became the hub of Islam.

Undoubtedly, Hazrat Khadijah (RA) was a remarkable woman who left her business to aid the underprivileged and those in need. She was also a brilliant leader with exceptional business and homemaking skills. By her choice, expertise, and assistance, Hazrat Khadijah (RA) demonstrated her dedication as a mother and friend, setting a high standard for women throughout history.

Life after Marriage to the Holy Prophet (PBUH)

Khadijah was indeed blessed and had already embraced Islam, turning away from idolatry. She held a great love for the Prophet (PBUH), and despite the means to delegate tasks to servants, she would always serve him herself. She was also a mother of six. After Zainab, Ruqayyah, Umm-kulthum, and Fatima (RA) came the first two sons.

The hadeeth recorded by Al-Bukhari describes how Hazrat Khadijah (RA) comforted Prophet Muhammad (PBUH) in his hour of need, supported him when no one else did, and helped him comprehend what had transpired by bringing him to Waraqa (her cousin). When it was not Farz (obligatory), Hazrat Khadijah (RA) and the Prophet (PBUH) would pray in private.

Hazrat Khadijah (RA) became the source of solace and ease for the Prophet (PBUH) and his family, even during this trying period. She spent 25 years in the company of Prophet Muhammad (PBUH). She died at the age of 65 in his tenth year of prophethood.

The Faithful Persecuted

Hazrat Khadijah (RA) was a great help to the Prophet (PBUH) during the early days of Islam. Her stature and renown caused the unbelievers to lessen their abuse of the Prophet (PBUH). She used to comfort him as they tortured him, explaining that their methods were ineffective and would not impact the Prophet (PBUH).

In the seventh year of the Prophet's life, the Quraish drove the Prophet (PBUH) and his entire family outside of Makkah, where they lived in abject poverty for three years. The adults were forced to eat tree leaves as their food supply ran out. Hazrat Khadijah's (RA) relatives covertly sent them food supplies during that period.

The Quraish, enraged by the rapid spread of Islam despite their vehement opposition, launched a vicious campaign to halt its growth. Muslims went through a trying time, yet they did not waver. They were sure that Islam would ultimately prevail, that Allah would assist them and that this time of trial would soon come to an end.

Through revelation, Allah comforted the Holy Prophet (PBUH) on multiple occasions, strengthening the faith of all Muslims. Among the most severely affected were the slaves, who faced intense persecution from their owners to force them to renounce Islam.

One such illustration is of one slave called Bilal (RA), who converted to Islam. On one such occasion, Bilal (RA) was led by his owner, Umayyah bin Khalaf, outside the town and forced to lie on his bare back in the intense sun. Then, massive stones were piled on top of his chest. He was occasionally hauled through Makkah's cobblestone streets. Then Umayyah would order him to abandon his faith and start singing praises to Laat and 'Uzzaa, the Makkah gods. Despite all of this torment, Bilal (RA) steadfastly proclaimed, "Ahad! Ahad! Ahad is one."

Another slave was Ammaar (RA). He was frequently abused physically and asked to give up Islam. Both his mother, Samiyyah (RA), and father, Yaasir (RA), suffered from torture.

> *Holy Prophet (PBUH) said: "Family of Yaasir! Bear up with patience, as your final resort is paradise." (Sunan Ibn Majah)*

After Hazrat Yaasir (RA) succumbed to his wounds shortly after, Abu Jahl used a spear to kill his wife, Hazrat Samiyyah (RA). A female slave called Zinnirah (RA) was beaten so severely by Abu Jahl that she lost her sight. Similar abuses were inflicted against other slaves.

It goes without saying that Hazrat Muhammad (PBUH), Hazrat Khadijah (RA), and other Muslims were horrified to see other Muslims being tortured. The treatment of the free citizens who converted to Islam was not any less brutal. They suffered various forms of torture from their chiefs and elders.

Zubairra bin 'Awwaam, the nephew of Hazrat Khadijah (RA), was frequently wrapped up in a rug, and smoke was forced through the mat to suffocate him and torment him. He bore the torment with patience, saying repeatedly that he would not deny the truth now that he had realised it.

The Quraish encouraged the petty individuals among them to harass the Prophet Muhammad (PBUH) in every manner imaginable. His foes used to throw trash at him and yell obscenities at him when he went out on the street.

His neighbours flung stones into his home, strewn thorns outside his door, and inserted offensive-smelling materials within his walls. Hazrat Khadijah (RA) and the Prophet Muhammad (PBUH) showed great patience in the face of this.

Supporting the Holy Prophet Muhammad (PBUH) required immense fortitude and dignity from Hazrat Khadijah (RA) and her family. Haarith, the son of Hazrat Khadijah (RA) and her first husband Abu Haallah gave his life to protect the Prophet Muhammad (PBUH). The Holy Prophet (PBUH) went to the Kabah and addressed the crowd there after receiving a directive from Allah to preach in public and said:

"Declare: 'There is none worthy of worship except Allah', and you will be successful." (Musnad Ahmad)

The Holy Prophet (PBUH) was attacked by the Quraish, who were present because they were deeply outraged. Upon learning this, Haarith hurried to defend the Prophet Muhammad (PBUH) and valiantly engaged the assailants. A Quraish person pulled out a sword and instantly killed Haarith. As a result, he suffered a martyr's death for Islam.

Naturally, Hazrat Khadijah (RA) was devastated by her son's passing, yet she accepted God's plan. When Hazrat Khadijah (RA) heard how cruelly the Makkah people treated the Prophet Muhammad (PBUH) and his adherents, she became upset.

The Muslims' life in Makkah was getting harder and harder every day. The Holy Prophet (PBUH) encouraged the community to relocate to Abyssinia. Hazrat Khadijah (RA) was deeply saddened to witness her nephew, son-in-law, and daughter depart Makkah for safety abroad.

Occasionally, the Holy Prophet (PBUH) would return home greatly disheartened and disillusioned by the Makkah people's rejection of his claim. Despite everything, she maintained her composure and consoled her spouse, family, and other believers during this trying time. The Holy Prophet (PBUH) always needs Hazrat Khadijah (RA) to comfort and uphold him. She was adamant that people would eventually embrace Islam and had great faith in Allah's assistance.

The Business Empire

Hazrat Khadijah (RA), the first Muslim woman, was a prominent and prosperous businesswoman in the Arab world. Hazrat Khadijah (RA), the woman of wonders, is one of the greatest inspirations in our lives. She was perceptive, bright, and clever. Without a question, of all the marriages that Prophet Muhammad (PBUH) had, Hazrat Khadijah (RA) was the most dependable and favoured.

Renowned and prosperous, Hazrat Khadijah (RA) was a business-woman of great repute. She inherited her father's abilities during a hazardous and predominately male era. When she took over the company, it was extremely difficult for her to assume this job and sell commodities through the main commercial routes of the times, which were Makkah, Syria, and Yemen. Her business was the most renowned, with a reputation for honest business practices and superi-or products, and it was bigger than all the Quraish trades put together.

Highlights of her Entrepreneurial Journey

The business endeavours of Hazrat Khadijah (RA) were distinguished by their inventiveness and insight. She made investments in long-distance commerce caravans, such as those that went to Yemen and Syria, which greatly increased her income and power. Hazrat Khadijah's (RA) commercial expertise also extended to the management of her vast agricultural holdings, which generated significant profits and created jobs for a large number of people.

Hazrat Khadijah's (RA) business endeavours grew quickly as a result of her ability to take advantage of Makkah's advantageous location along trade routes that link Arabia with its neighbours. Hazrat Khadijah (RA) made trading easier for things like luxury goods, textiles, and spices, forming profitable alliances with traders across the Arabian Peninsula.

By venturing into new markets and broadening her range of economic ventures, Hazrat Khadijah (RA) exhibited ingenuity beyond conventional trading routes. She invested in various sectors, including manufacturing, real estate, and agriculture, taking advantage of new opportunities and adjusting to shifting market conditions.

Hazrat Khadijah (RA) was credited with securing advantageous agreements and using shrewd negotiation strategies for her economic success. She developed close bonds with her trading partners, gaining their respect and trust through ethical business practices. Her reputation for honesty and dependability facilitated the expansion of Hazrat Khadijah's (RA) economic empire.

She had a strong sense of social responsibility and her Islamic faith guided her charitable endeavours. She donated part of her fortune to help the widows, orphans, and impoverished people of Makkah society. Her giving was not limited to money; she gave those in need clothing, food, and shelter as well.

Hazrat Khadijah (RA) was a devoted supporter of the welfare of the Muslim community and the advancement of Islam, in addition to helping those in need. She kindly provided funding for missions to propagate Islam and protect the Muslim Ummah, including those led by the Holy Prophet Muhammad (PBUH).

The charitable endeavours of Hazrat Khadijah (RA) were crucial in enabling marginalised groups—women in particular—by giving them chances for financial independence and self-sufficiency. To empower women to support their families and make a living, she founded microfinance programmes and vocational training programmes.

The business endeavours of Hazrat Khadijah (RA) are a timeless inspiration for ambitious entrepreneurs, especially women, who want to build long-lasting companies. Her clever handling of trade caravans, wise investments, and dedication to moral business conduct are all important lessons for contemporary business owners aiming to succeed in a cutthroat international marketplace.

Hazrat Khadijah's (RA) leadership attributes, such as her strategic decision-making, visionary leadership, and dedication to servant leadership, provide important insights for modern leaders in the public and private sectors. In today's complicated and interconnected world, her emphasis on consensus-building, inclusivity, and collaboration serves as a paradigm for ethical leadership and effective administration.

Islamic finance, including ethical investment, was made possible by Khadijah's (RA) commitment to fair trade ideals and ethical business practices. Her focus on fairness, honesty, and integrity in business dealings is in line with current initiatives to advance socially conscious investing, ethical finance, and environmentally friendly banking methods. The economic model of Hazrat Khadijah (RA) provides Islamic financial institutions with important insights for maintaining ethical standards and Shariah compliance in their operations.

Hazrat Khadijah (RA) provided essential economic services to modern society since she was a living example of ethical enterprise, social responsibility, and gender equality. Hazrat Khadijah's (RA) economic services are still in demand in today's world because they provide timeless wisdom and useful ideas for dealing with current issues. Through the entrepreneurship, social responsibility, and ethical values of Hazrat Khadijah (RA), individuals and organisations can support social justice, gender equality, and sustainable economic development in the contemporary world.

Hazrat Khadijah (RA), a formidable community leader who bravely refused to back down in the face of extreme abuse, is an inspiration to modern-day women and men. She is a prosperous businesswoman, a spouse, a mother, and a role model. Hazrat Khadijah (RA), a protector of the helpless and orphaned and a giver to the underprivileged, embodies the ideals we uphold today and the reality we work to achieve.

Not only is Hazrat Khadijah (RA) a model woman, but she is also a model human being. Her qualities are admirable and should be emulated by both men and women. She is a living example of outstanding leadership, courage, strength, achievement, devotion, and compassion, which are crucial to the continuous fight for gender equality.

Services to Islam

Following her marriage to the Prophet (PBUH), she passed on all of her money to him, fully aware of how much he would require this wealth for Islam in the very near future.

Over the course of fifteen years, the Prophet Muhammad (PBUH) and Hazrat Khadijah (RA) did not spend a significant amount of these riches for themselves.

The Prophet (PBUH) came to the realisation that he was a prophet after a period of fifteen years, during which he led a tranquil life. The inhabitants of Makkah, particularly the Quraish, turned out to be his most formidable adversaries. As a result, they made his life and the lives of his associates extremely challenging.

The reason for this was because he was left alone. During this crucial period, his uncle Abu Talib and, of course, his wife Hazrat Khadijah (RA) were the two individuals who supported him the most deeply.

Hazrat Khadijah (RA) was of assistance to the Prophet of Islam in two different ways. The first thing that happened was that the people of Makkah had to go through a lot of difficulties in order to accept the invitation that the Prophet extended to them to become Muslims. They were unable to make enough money to purchase the food and resources they needed on a daily basis. It was necessary for the Prophet to carry out this task for them.

Additionally, to travel to Abyssinia, a number of the newly converted Muslims were required to depart from Makkah. Money was necessary for all of this. It was Hazrat Khadijah (RA) who generously contributed the funds. Her wealth was also put toward the liberation of slaves.

One could ponder whether or not Islam would have been able to endure in the absence of Hazrat Khadijah (RA)'s wealth.

She is the only person who can be compared to Hazrat Abu Talib, who used his power as the head of his clan to help the Prophet (PBUH), and Ali, who used his sword for Islam. Her contribution to Islam is comparable to both of these individuals. "No property has ever been so useful to me as Hazrat Khadijah (RA)'s," the Prophet (PBUH) would say, and "Religion (Islam) succeeded only through Ali's sword and Hazrat Khadijah (RA)'s wealth." Both of these statements were frequently spoken by the Prophet.

Second, she supported his assertion that he was the Prophet and urged him to continue his mission. She believed in his claim. Whenever he required her assistance, she was there for him. When he went to pray at the Kaaba, she accompanied him and worshipped behind him. When his adversaries smeared dirt on him, she assisted him in cleaning himself. She made sure to nurture him whenever he was hurt.

During the time that he was forced to relocate to the estate of Hazrat Abu Talib after being shunned by the Quraish, she accompanied him in order to provide him with care and assistance throughout his life.

She suffered from starvation and tiredness for the duration of her three-year stay there, and she passed away shortly after the conclusion of the boycott.

It is because Allah placed such a high value on her sacrifices for Islam that he acknowledges them in the Quran:

"And He found you poor and made [you] self-sufficient."
(Quran 93:8)

And he discovered you in a state of need and made you self-sufficient (by means of money).

In addition, when she was still alive, Allah would send her salaams. Jibril approached the Prophet (PBUH) and addressed him with the words:

"O Messenger of Allah! Your name is Hazrat Khadijah (RA). It appears that she has arrived with a bowl of soup made of food or drink. When she arrives to you, please extend greetings to her from both her Lord (Allah) and from me. As a result of the subsequent occurrence, it was established that she was granted a very high place in Paradise upon her passing." (Sahih Bukhari and Sahih Muslim)

Immediately upon the passing of Lady Hazrat Khadijah (RA), Hazrat Fatima (AS), who was only a child at the time, inquired of the Prophet (PBUH), "Where is my mother?"

"Your Lord commands you to inform Fatima that Allah sends His blessings to her, and He also says: 'Your mother is in a special house (in heaven), the corners of which are made of gold and the poles of which are of rubies,'" said the Angel Jibril before he could answer her.

"Your mother is in a house that is made of gold and rubies. It is situated in the middle of the residences that belong to Mariam and Asiya."

Even the Prophet (PBUH) acknowledged and appreciated Hazrat Khadijah's (RA) contributions to Islam throughout his life. Every time he thought about her after she had passed away, he did so with tears in his eyes and praise on his tongue. In the presence of Aisha, the Prophet (PBUH) once repeated the name of Lady Hazrat Khadijah (RA).

This irritated Aisha, and she responded by saying, "She was an old lady, and Allah replaced her with a better one for you." The words that Aisha had spoken infuriated the Prophet (PBUH), and he responded by saying, "Allah did not give me (any other wife) better than she." "Despite the fact that others did not accept me, she did. When other people had doubts about me, she believed me. During times when others kept their wealth away from me, she shared it with me, and Allah only gave me children via her."

When Hazrat Khadijah (RA) was still alive, the Prophet did not marry another woman. This was the final honour bestowed upon her in recognition of her contributions to Islam at the time. At that moment, he focused all of his attention on her.

According to Tabari, a well-known Sunni scholar, the Prophet Muhammad (PBUH) was known to laud Hazrat Khadijah (RA) by saying,

"The best women of Paradise are Hazrat Khadijah (RA) (daughter of Khuwailid); Maryam, the daughter of Imran; Fatima, the daughter of Muhammad (PBUH); and Asiya, the daughter of Mudaim, the wife of Pharoah."

Chapter Three

Umm Salamah: Wisdom and Wealth

Hazrat Umm Salamah, What a fascinating life she led! Hind was her real name. She was the daughter of Abu Umaiyyah Hudhayfah ibn al Mugheerah, a member of the Quraish clan from Bani Makhzoom, who was known as "Zad ar-Rakib," or the Provision of the Traveller, for his extraordinary hospitality and kindness to the visitors.

Hazrat Umm Salamah was endowed with a noble and generous upbringing, as well as intelligence, learning, wisdom, skill, and beauty in both appearance and character. Her contributions to pre-Islamic society serve as an example of strength, discernment, and commitment to Islamic values. Let's examine her life in more detail.

From Wealth to Widowhood

Early Life and Marriages

Hazrat Umm-e-Salamah (RA) was a knowledgeable and competent woman from an honourable and reputable household. As one of the first women to migrate to Medina, she was among the first to join Islam. Before her, very few people had converted to Islam.

What earned the father of Hazrat Umm Salamah the title "provision of the traveller"? It was said he never allowed anyone travelling with him to bring their own supplies. No matter how many there were or how far they had to travel, he would rather be in charge of that. Thus, Hind was born and reared in this firmly established household full of bravery and charity. She nourished herself with its clear spring water until she was full, and then she grew to become a fragrant, blossoming branch that bore a lovely fruit. She had a beautiful appearance and demeanour, and she was intelligent.

The Quran highlights the esteemed status of those early Muslims who embraced the faith and undertook the migration, showing the high regard in which Allah holds them.

> *As Allah says: "And the first forerunners [in the faith] among the Muhajireen (the Emigrants) and the Ansar (the Helpers) and those who followed them with good conduct - Allah is pleased with them, and they are pleased with Him, and He has prepared for them gardens beneath which rivers flow, wherein they will abide forever. That is the great attainment." (Quran 9:100)*

Hazrat Umm-e-Salamah (RA), a matriarchal young woman, married Hazrat Abdullah (RA) bin Abdil Asad (Abu Salamah) when she was in her teens. Her two half-brothers were Makhzum cousins to Abdullah. As a privileged couple, they were required to uphold tradition by submitting to the family gods and joining Makkah's hierarchical structure.

However, the young couple found resonance in the Prophet's words. When their parents learned that their children had joined Muhammad's (PBUH) infamous group, they were just as shocked as when they had first rejoiced over the couple's marriage. Abu Salamah (RA) was renowned for his honesty, bravery, kindness, endurance, and patience.

About Abu Salamah, the Prophet (PBUH) had once said:
"He will be the first person to be given his record of deeds
on the Day of Judgement." (Sahih Muslim)

Tragedy and Resilience

During the Age of Ignorance, women were viewed as immature beings who should be kept out of social situations. They were not fighters and required special protection because if they were captured by the enemy, they would become servants and cause shame and humiliation to their tribe. Even if they were rescued, they would still face excessive humiliation from their own people. It was extremely difficult for clans and tribes engaged in war, migration, or both to protect a woman.

On the other hand, some women were valued and acknowledged due to their characteristics. However, the advent of the Prophet Muhammad (PBUH) gave women a new identity. As a result, women were granted a unique position in society; some of these ladies were the Prophet's wives. Hazrat Umm Salamah (RA) played a vital role in Islamic history as the most well-known wife after Lady Hazrat Khadijah (RA).

They endured a particularly frustrating period while they were residents of Makkah, where they faced persecution and oppression for simply embracing Islam. However, Allah (SWT) bestowed Iman (faith) upon them, and they persisted, battled, and endeavoured with their Islam in Makkah.

Migration Period

She performed the first migration to Abyssinia with her husband, making them two of the first Muslims. It was also claimed that she was the first female immigrant. Together with her husband, Abū Salamah (RA), Hazrat Umm Salamah (RA) made her first hijrah to Ethiopia, where the

King—who would subsequently convert to Islam—accepted Muslims seeking safety from Makkah persecution.

After Umar (RA) and Ḥamzah (RA), two influential members of Makkah society, converted to Islam, several Muslims thought Makkah would be friendlier and left for home. However, they were wrong. Even while Muslims in Ethiopia led comfortable lives, some of them still missed their native country.

Muslims moved to Medina after experiencing more persecution, receiving a kind offer from a nearby clan, and divine approval to relocate. This time, a greater number of them departed Makkah. The journey's difficulty varied widely: some bravely departed, while others were restrained by their families. Among those halted on their way out were Hazrat Umm Salamah, her husband, and her child.

She says in her own words: "When Abu Salamah (my husband) decided to leave for Medina, he prepared a camel for me, hoisted me on it, and placed our son Salamah on my lap. My husband then took the lead and went on without stopping or waiting for anything. Before we were out of Makkah, some men from the clan stopped us and said to my husband: 'Though you are free to do what you like with yourself, you have no power over your wife. She is our daughter. Do you expect us to allow you to take her away from us?' They then pounced on him and snatched me away from him. My husband's clan, Banu Abdul-Asad, saw them taking both me and my child and they became hot with rage. 'No! By Allah,' they shouted, 'we shall not abandon the boy. He is our son, and we have first claim over him.' They took him by the hand and pulled him away from me. Suddenly, in the space of a few moments, I found myself alone and lonely." (Ibn Ishaq)

It is the hardest separation for the sake of Allah, who never loses a good deed. Allah declares: "

> *"Indeed, we shall not make the reward of anyone who does his [righteous] deeds in the most perfect manner to be lost." (Quran 18: 30)*

Since she converted to Islam, Hazrat Umm Salamah dedicated her life to Allah! Even in her worst situations, she felt Allah's presence and support. He envelops the sceptics from behind. For anybody who goes to Him in repentance and depends on Him, He is the greatest Helper.

Every day, Hazrat Umm Salamah (RA) would cry because she longed to be with her husband, the Muslims, and the Prophet Muhammad (PBUH). She persisted in Makkah, pleading and arguing with them to allow her to leave.

When her requests were finally granted, she left for Medina with her young child in tow. However, Allah the Exalted guarded her for the day-long voyage, which took place in a vast and isolated desert dotted with mountains, lowlands, and sand hills where raptors and reptiles were waiting for their victims. She did not feel anxious or terrified.

During her journey, a man by the name of 'Uthman ibn Ṭalḥah (RA) asked her about her travels. Realising the dangers she faced travelling alone with a child, he chose to accompany her for protection.

> *Hazrat Umm Salamah said about 'Uthman, "I have, by Allah, never met an Arab more generous and noble than he." (Ibn Kathir)*

Then, the large family—or rather, the little family—was reunited. It was modest in terms of the number of members it had, but it was significant in terms of the historical movement it created its Jihad, and its global reach.

Finally reunited, Abu Salamah (RA) and Hazrat Umm Salamah (RA) could spend their lives together happily. Mutual affection and generosity characterised their bond, which was strong. She did not lose trust in the wake of this occurrence. She wept over her loss, but her conviction remained unwavering.

> *In the Quran, Allah says: "And whosoever fears Allah and keeps his duty to Him, He will make a way for him to get out [from every difficulty]. And He will provide him from [sources] he never could imagine, and whosoever puts his trust in Allah, then He will suffice him. Verily, Allah will accomplish his purpose. Indeed, Allah has set a measure for all things." (Quran 65: 2-3)*

When one door closed, another opened shortly after. She left her issues in the hands of Allah and relied on Him to safeguard her and her baby while travelling alone. Because she believed that Allah had changed her family members' hearts and permitted them to let her depart, she persevered in her good intentions, and Allah sent her assistance.

Hazrat Umm Salamah (RA) recalled something the Prophet (PBUH) said to Abu Salamah (RA) one day when they were sitting together in their house.

> *"Whoever is married on earth will be married in paradise." she said, "Let's make a pact not to remarry after death so we can be in paradise together." (Tabarani)*

After listening to this, Abu Salamah (RA), in his kindness, love, and wisdom, answered:

> *"No, when I die, marry someone else." He then directed his words to God and prayed, "After I'm gone, bless her with someone who is better and will not make her sad or do her harm." (Sahih Muslim)*

Later, Abu Salamah (RA) suffered a combat wound and passed away, becoming a martyr. The Prophet (PBUH) said the following when he closed his eyes and prayed over his body on his deathbed:

> *"When the soul is taken away, the sight follows it." (Sahih Muslim)*

He then said:

> *"Oh Allah, forgive Abu Salamah, raise his degree among those who are rightly guided, grant him a successor in his descendants. Forgive us and him, O Lord of the Universe, and make his grave spacious, and grant him light in it." (Sahih Muslim)*

After some time, Hazrat Abu Bakr As-Siddiq (RA) approached Um Salamah (RA) with a proposal, but she turned him down. Then, when Hazrat Umar (RA) proposed, she likewise declined. Then, the Prophet (PBUH) proposed to Um Salamah (RA).

When the Prophet (PBUH) sent her a marriage proposal, she initially turned it down, citing three reasons: first, she was so well-cared for and loved by Abu Salamah (RA) that she was afraid that, in her piqued temper, she would be impolite to the Prophet (PBUH) and forfeit the rewards for any good deeds she might have done; second, she was no longer a young woman; and third, she had children.

The Prophet (PBUH) gave a profound and elegant response to this. He promised to pray, and in the name of Allah, she would learn to control her temper. He (PBUH) stated that he, too, was an old man, and when it came to children, that is precisely why he asked her to marry him—he wanted to be their protector.

The Prophet (PBUH) said: "Allah has commanded me to marry only with the women of Paradise." Hazrat Umm Salamah participated in the Ridwan pledge; therefore, she deserved Paradise." (Ibn Sa'd)

Thus, four years after Hijrah, in the month of Shawwal, Abu Salamah's (RA) final petition was answered, and she (RA) joined the Prophet's (PBUH) household.

Her Business Activities

In addition, Hazrat Umm Salamah (RA) was a learned and sharp lady who dedicated her life to serving the underprivileged. Her life story demonstrates how crucial it is for women to advise wisely and impact important family decisions. She was well known for her intelligence, grace, and wisdom.

Prophet Muhammad's (PBUH) esteemed companion, Hazrat Umm Salamah (RA), actively participated in commercial dealings. Her life is an example of how a fulfilling profession and family obligations can coexist. Let's have a look!

Her Contribution as an Entrepreneur

Hazrat Umm Salamah (RA) was a widow of considerable means before her marriage to the Prophet Muhammad (PBUH). She inherited property and wealth from her first husband, Abu Salamah (RA). Her management of these assets would have involved careful handling and potential investment to ensure their continued benefit for her family and the community.

Her guidance and influence could have encouraged fair and ethical business practices among the Muslim traders in Medina, thereby fostering a healthy trading environment. As one of the Prophet's wives, Hazrat Umm Salamah (RA) would have been well-versed in the ethical teachings of Islam regarding trade and commerce.

Hazrat Umm Salamah (RA) was known for her generosity and charitable activities. In the early Muslim community, charity often involved financial transactions and investments to support the poor and needy. By distributing wealth in such a manner, she contributed to Medina's economic stability and social welfare.

A scholar among scholars, Hazrat Umm Salamah was. Hazrat Umm Salamah was so knowledgeable about the Quran and its translation that even 'Abdullah bin 'Abbas, one of the first scholars of the Quran, would come to her for advice on Islamic law. She recounted over 300 hadiths and was regarded as one of the companions with the best judgement on Islamic law, and from her writings, some of which provided guidelines on economic and trade practices.

However, Hazrat Umm Salamah's (RA) field of skill extended beyond the understanding of Islam. She was a master of writing and an expressive speaker. She used carefully considered words and phrases that were ideal for expressing the concepts she was expressing when she spoke. Her writing style was appropriate for artistic expression.

Her role as a prominent female figure in the community likely empowered other women to engage in economic activities, including trade and investment. Her example would have encouraged women to manage their finances effectively and participate in the city's economic life.

Hazrat Umm Salamah's (RA) overall contributions to the economic environment in Medina can be inferred through her influence, charitable actions, and guidance based on Islamic principles. Her role in shaping a fair and ethical community indirectly supported the growth and stability of trade and investments in early Islamic society.

Contributions to Islamic Knowledge

Hazrat Umm Salamah (RA), Muhammad's (PBUH) wife, was a leader. She was articulate, knowledgeable, and unafraid to speak her mind. Her encounter with Umar ibn al-Khattab (RA) is a testament to her strong character and assertiveness in defending the rights and dignity of the Prophet's (PBUH) household.

In this incident, Hazrat Umm Salamah (RA) confronted Hazrat Umar (RA) when he was interfering in the affairs of the Prophet's (PBUH) wives. Her actions were not merely confrontational but also impactful. The Arabic phrase "kasara" used to describe her effect on Hazrat Umar (RA) conveys that she deeply affected him, almost shaking him out of his state of agitation and causing him to reconsider his actions. This reflects her ability to speak truth to power and assertively defend the boundaries and rights of the Prophet's (PBUH) family.

This demonstrates her fortitude and capacity to deal with challenging individuals. Hazrat Umm Salamah (RA) possessed self-control. She strengthened her inner life by keeping the midnight optional prayers and fasting on Mondays, Thursdays, and Fridays. She was a knowledgeable and trustworthy woman in Muhammad's (PBUH) life.

Her Wisdom Highlights

She was well-liked and recognised by the women as "Hazrat Umm Salamah (RA) the Wise." The most well-known tale of her wisdom is the Agreement of Hudaybiyya, which took place at a pivotal point in Muhammad's (PBUH) life when he signed a peace agreement with the Makkah chiefs.

His supporters were offended by the proceedings because they believed Muhammad (PBUH) had compromised too much during negotiations. Then, he felt inspired to urge the group to commit to one another more deeply. Every man made a promise. However, the sensation of that shared moment of confidence was quickly gone.

They were put to greater trials by the Makkah people, and they objected when Muhammad (PBUH) signed a peace agreement that appeared to offer the pilgrims very little in exchange for their vow to cancel their trip to Makkah that year. Then, much like they were doing the hajj, he instructed them to carry out the ceremonial sacrifice.

He turned to Hazrat Umm Salamah (RA) for guidance during this crisis. She said:

> *"Prophet of God, do you approve of this? Go out and speak not a word to any of them until you have slaughtered your fattened camel and summoned your shaver to shave your hair." (Sahih Bukhari)*

The startled atmosphere was shattered as the people witnessed Muhammad (PBUH) perform the tasks he had given them. Revelation confirmed the Messenger's strategy with the chapter of Victory (Quran 48:1–29).

"Allah sent down sakina (tranquil presence) into the hearts of those who stay true to a trust (the mumin), that they may add faith to their faith..." (Quran 48:4)

Thus, it may be claimed that Hazrat Umm Salamah (RA) spent a critical period discussing and approving a significant peace agreement. The Prophet, who was taken aback by the sudden change in circumstances, was probably most relieved by her counsel.

He had always known that his dear friends would follow his orders with all of their love and devotion. It was just unthinkable to witness them disobeying his commands three times. She did everything she could to give him the best counsel as a faithful wife. This was known about Hazrat Umm Salamah (RA) even before her union with the Prophet.

Hazrat Umm Salamah (RA) was regarded as having a great deal of insight. Hazrat Aisha (RA) recounts that the Prophet conferred with her multiple times. People do not naturally possess wisdom. It grows with time, is shaped by challenges and experiences in life, and is intimately connected to how we see the world. She continued to counsel the populace with her extraordinary wisdom and discernment until her passing at 84. Many scholars consulted her for advice on Shariah issues even after the Prophet (PBUH) passed away and respected her analysis of legal and business matters.

Role in Islamic Jurisprudence

Hazrat Umm Salamah (RA) contributed significantly and in a variety of ways to the growth of Islamic law. Her services included narrating hadith, issuing legal rulings (fatwas), advocating for women's rights, and spearheading educational initiatives within the early Muslim community. She was regarded as one of the most esteemed wives of the Prophet Muhammad (PBUH). Together, their contributions impacted how Islamic law and morality were developed.

Hazrat Umm Salamah's (RA) vast narration of the Hadiths, which are fundamental sources of Islamic ethics and law, is one of her most significant contributions to Islamic jurisprudence. Understanding the real-world applicability of the Quran and the teachings of the Prophet (PBUH) requires a comprehension of these hadiths.

Her narratives touch on a wide range of subjects, including commerce, social conduct, family law, and religious rites. Hazrat Umm Salamah (RA) was instrumental in guaranteeing that the teachings of Islam were accurately transmitted to the coming generations by preserving and transmitting these teachings.

Apart from her function as a hadith narrator, Hazrat Umm Salamah (RA) was also a well-respected legal expert. She relied on her intimate knowledge of Islamic law and her deep connection with the Prophet to provide multiple legal opinions, or fatwas, on a variety of topics.

Her views were respected because they were perceptive and true to the ideals of equity and justice. This admiration for her legal knowledge highlighted her important contribution to the growth of Islamic jurisprudence, especially in family law and women's rights.

Hazrat Umm Salamah (RA) was a fervent supporter of women's rights as they applied to Islamic law. She gave advice on matters including inheritance, marriage, and divorce with the goal of upholding women's rights and treating them fairly.

Her activism promoted the idea that women's participation and voices were essential in the understanding and execution of Islamic principles, helping to develop a more inclusive and just strategy within Islamic law.

In addition to her work in activism and law, Hazrat Umm Salamah (RA) was a committed teacher and mentor. Her position as an educator was crucial for promoting a culture of study and inquiry within the Islamic tradition.

Hazrat Umm Salamah (RA) aided in the spiritual and intellectual growth of early Muslim society by imparting knowledge to others. She helped a great deal of people—including other women—understand Islamic law and religious customs. Her educational initiatives made it possible for a larger portion of society to interact with and understand Islamic jurisprudence and helped spread important knowledge about Islam.

Her guidance demonstrated a thorough awareness of Islamic beliefs and strategic thinking, which contributed to securing a peaceful conclusion amid a potentially conflicting situation. Her capacity to apply Islamic principles to practical situations was demonstrated by her participation, which further cemented her influence on the development of Islamic jurisprudence.

In sum, Hazrat Umm Salamah (RA) made significant and wide-ranging contributions to Islamic law. She significantly influenced the development of early Islam's moral and legal system by narrating hadith. Her contributions to the growth of Islamic jurisprudence have endured, as seen by how her legacy continues to influence Islamic law and practice.

Chapter Four

Asma Bint Abu Bakr: The Resourceful Trader

Early Life and Family Influence

The history of Islam is filled with the sacrifices made by the companions of the Prophet (PBUH). Among the early Muslims, Hazrat Asma Bint Abu Bakr (RA) holds a particular place in history. She has made many sacrifices for Islam.

Hazrat Asma (RA) is the daughter of Hazrat Abu Bakr Al Siddiq (RA), the first man to accept Islam and the Prophet's (PBUH) closest friend and companion after his first wife, Khadijah (RA). Prior to Islam, Hazrat Asma's (RA) parents were divorced. Her mother, Qutailah, stayed a polytheist even though her father was the first man to convert to Islam. In addition, Aisha bint Abi Bakr (RA), the mother of the believers, was an elder sister of Hazrat Asma (RA).

Out of the fifteen people, Hazrat Asma (RA) was the seventeenth to accept Islam. She vowed allegiance to the Prophet (PBUH) and maintained her faith in him. When Qutailah, Hazrat Asma's (RA) mother, visited her in Medina, she brought gifts for her daughter, including dates. Before allowing her mother to enter the house or receive the presents, Hazrat Asma (RA) dispatched her sister Hazrat Aisha (RA) to ask the Prophet Muhammad (PBUH) if it was appropriate for her to extend hospitality to her non-Muslim mother.

She said in her own words: "My mother came to me while she was a nonbeliever during the lifetime of the Prophet (PBUH). I asked him (PBUH) about her. I said (seeking his verdict), My mother has come to me, and she desires to receive a reward from me, shall I keep good relations with her?" (Sahih Muslim & Bukhari)

In response to this, the Holy Prophet (PBUH) said:

"Yes, keep good relation with her." (Sahih Bukhari)

Hazrat Asma (RA) was a major factor in the Holy Prophet's (PBUH) journey from Makkah to Medina. Hazrat Asma (RA) was to provide food to Abu Bakr (RA) and the Prophet (PBUH), who were sheltering in Cave Thawr. It was around three kilometres from the cave on a mountain route.

She carried meals every day for three days despite being seven months pregnant. On the last day, Hazrat Asma (RA) organised their water skin and travel essentials; no rope was available to bind them when packing. She divided her Nitaq, or waist belt, in half and used one of the halves to fasten the bag. In recognition of this, she was given the honorific Zu Nataqin, which translates to "the lady of two belts."

The Prophet (PBUH) commended her for her deed of compassion and remarked to her: "Indeed, Allah has given you, in exchange for this girdle, two belts in Paradise." (Sahih Bukhari)

Her Initial Challenges

Hazrat Asma was a very noble, devoted, wise, and patient woman. She came from a well-known Muslim household, grew up in a pure and devoted environment, and had an intimate relationship with the Prophet (PBUH) from a very young age. After the Prophet's passing, her father, Hazrat Abu Bakr al Siddiq (RA), became the first Khalifah and a close friend of the prophet.

One of the Prophet Muhammad's (PBUH) special personal assistants was her spouse, Zubayr ibn al-Awwam. Abdullah ibn az-Zubayr, her son, rose to prominence due to his unwavering adherence to Truth and incorruptibility. Ten years older than Hazrat Aisha (RA), Hazrat Asma was extremely young when she accepted the Prophet's (PBUH) message. As late as 14 years old, Hazrat Asma (RA) was the messenger of the Prophet (PBUH). Before her, only roughly seventeen people, both men and women, converted to Islam.

Hazrat Asma (RA) was eventually faced by Abu Jahil, the most powerful and influential man in Makkah and the greatest enemy of Islam during that period, before her own hijrah to Medina. Hazrat Asma (RA) bravely and fearlessly refused to cede and withheld any knowledge concerning Hazrat Abu Bakr (RA) and Hazrat Muhammad (PBUH) despite three attempts to ask her where her father and the Prophet (PBUH) were.

Alone in a city encircled by Islam's adversaries, she was faced by the man pursuing the Prophet (PBUH). Abu Jahil gave her such a severe slap across the face that her earring came loose. To get to the Prophet, Abu Jahil had killed Muslims in public one after the other. She kept the secret, bravely and tolerantly enduring the suffering.

The height of Muslim bravery and female strength was the bravery she displayed while carrying a child in the face of an adversary.

She was devoted to standing by the Prophet (PBUH) and her father despite all the difficulties and threats she encountered at the time. Throughout her life, she demonstrated selflessness and sacrifice. She was crucial in supporting her father and the Holy Prophet (PBUH) during the Muslim migration from Makkah to Medina on another occasion. All of this demonstrates her bravery.

Hazrat Asma (RA) went with the Prophet's (PBUH) daughters when they were invited to Quba, near Medina. When they were close to Quba, she gave birth to her child, Abdullah bin Zubair. The Holy Prophet (PBUH) took the infant in his lap and put a piece of date that he had chewed in the child's mouth. Abdullah was the first child born to Muhajirin in Medina.

She initially went through a difficult period because her husband, Zubair ibn Al-Awwam, left everything in Makkah and moved to Medina penniless. The wealthy man's daughter was forced to care for animals, knead, grind, and get water.

During the Battle of Uhud, Hazrat Asma (RA) helped the Muslim forces by raising morale. She provided medical assistance and drinking water to keep the soldiers hydrated.

The true measure of Hazrat Asma's (RA) endurance and forbearance emerged following Hussein ibn Ali's (AS) martyrdom at Karbala. By then, she was close to ninety years old. Following the Karbala disaster, her son Abdullah bin Zubair, regarded as a wise, strong, and courageous man, drew large crowds of people.

He was successful in gaining Medina and Makkah's support. In due course, Hazrat Abdullah (RA) established his dominance over Iraq, the Hijaz, southern Arabia, most of Syria, and portions of Egypt.

Before the battle against Abdul Malik bin Marwan, the ruler of Damascus, Hazrat Asma (RA) gave her son advice, telling him that she would only mourn him if he died for a pointless and unfair cause:

"Death with honour is better than a life of peace with dishonour."(Al-Tabari)

Hazrat Abdullah (RA) charged into battle against Hajaj bin Yusuf, the commander of Marwan, and continued to fight until he was killed. He was beheaded, and his body was hung on a tree by the ruthless Hajaj.

"Hazrat Asma (RA) alone should take down his body," he declared. She needs to approach me and request my approval. She declined to go. In due course, Hajaj came to her and asked, "What do you say about this matter?" *She boldly replied, "Verily, you have destroyed him, and you have ruined his life, and with that, you have ruined your Hereafter." (Ibn Hisham)*

She further stated that she had heard the Prophet Muhammad (PBUH) state that: "A man would appear from the tribe of Banu Thaqif who would be a liar and a cruel and ignoble barbarian. Today, she has seen him for herself." (Musnad Ahmad)

Hajaj bin Yusuf left silently. Hajaj later dumped the body in the cemetery. She made arrangements for her son to be bathed, have a funeral prayer, and be buried in Makkah with her hands.

For all Muslim women, Asma bint Abu Bakr serves as an inspiration, and she is a symbol of bravery for all ages. She demonstrated that a woman can fight with men in combat and stand by her father as a son would.

Hazrat Asma (RA) Qualities

Hazrat Asma (RA) gained notoriety for her sharp mind and noble and exquisite attributes. She was a very giving individual.

Her son once said, "I have not seen two women more generous than my aunt Aisha and my mother Hazrat Asma. But their generosity was expressed in different ways. My aunt would accumulate one thing after another until she had gathered what she felt was sufficient and then distributed it all to those in need. My mother, on the other hand, would not keep anything even for the morrow." (Sahih Bukhari)

Seeing Hazrat Asma's (RA) composure under pressure was remarkable. It was a true testament to her high degree of knowledge, loyalty and dependability. Her father took all his wealth—roughly six thousand dirhams—with him when he fled Makkah, leaving nothing for his family. Abu Quhafah, the blind father of Hazrat Abu Bakr (RA), went to his home upon hearing of his leaving and told Hazrat Asma (RA), "I understand that he has left you bereft of money after he himself has abandoned you."

But Hazrat Asma (RA) remained silent. "No, grandfather; in fact, he has left us a sizable inheritance," she retorted. She collected a few pebbles and placed them in the little alcove in the wall where the money had been kept.

"Look how much money he has left us," she exclaimed, tossing a cloth over the pile and taking her grandfather's hand. Using this tactic, Hazrat Asma (RA) kept her father's business confidential and eased his anxieties, preventing him from handing them any of his personal money. This was due to her distaste for accepting help from a disbeliever of Islam, regardless of whether it was her grandfather.

Hazrat Asma (RA) was extremely sensitive, devoted, and patient. Zubair Bin Awam (RA), a companion of Hazrat Muhammad (PBUH), and Asma (RA) were married. Despite not coming from an affluent background, he was a genuinely nice man.

When Hazrat Asma (RA) married him, he was a poor man, but she faced financial difficulties as well. Yet, she did not moan and put forth much effort to support her husband. She used to bring water, bake bread, and feed the horse.

She has always shown her spouse a great deal of loyalty and respect. She and her spouse put in a great deal of work together till their impoverished circumstances eventually improved.

Hazrat Asma (RA) was a formidable and astute lady known for her strong mental and emotional strength. She even took part in one of the most iconic battles in Islamic history, the Battle of Yarmook, where Muslim women and children battled with incredible bravery and zeal.

As a key figure, she was one of the key players in the fall of the Byzantine Empire.

Her Wisdom in Balancing Business, Family & Principles

Once, a person came to Hazrat Asma (RA) and said:

> *"Mother of Abdullah, I am someone in need, and I intend to establish a business under the shadow of your house." Is my house the only location in Medina where a business can be started?" She inquired, saying, "You come and make a request of it when Zubair Bin Awam (RA) is also present there because if I grant you approval, my husband may not agree to that."*

Zubair bin Awam (RA) questioned, "Why is it that you forbid the destitute man from starting a business here?" after learning of Hazrat Asma's denial. What transpired next was described by Hazrat Asma as follows: "He created a business and made so much money that we sold our slave girl to him. I was sitting with the money in my lap when Az-Zubair appeared. 'Give this to me,' he commanded. '(I intend) to spend it in charity,' I declared"
(Ibn Sa'd)

Observe how Hazrat Asma (RA) supported letting that individual launch a company beneath their roof, but she disliked taking any action that would irritate or offend her husband. Therefore, she asked her husband a question to get his view. When he responded favourably, she accepted the proposition to launch a business in their home.

Eventually, Hazrat Asma's husband rose from early adversity and poverty to become one of the Sahabah's wealthiest men, but she refused to let this compromise her moral standards.

After her son Abdullah reached adulthood, Hazrat Asma moved in with her son's family after Al Zubair had divorced her. "The Girl of Two Belts" led a respectable and dignified life. She was often the object of Prophet Muhammad's (PBUH) constant prayers.

Later in life, she developed a growth on her neck. Several times, Prophet Muhammad (PBUH) caressed the oedema and begged God to keep her safe. She made a full recovery. She was strong because of Allah's (SWT) protection and carried this strength into the end. Her advanced age had not diminished her mental acuity or sharpness.

But in her old age, Hazrat Asma (RA) faced two calamities that put her to the test. The first was becoming blind, much like her grandfather, which left the once-independent woman in a dependent position.

The second trial was far more challenging and occurred during a pivotal time in Islamic history. In fact, one of the most memorable occasions in the early history of Islam was her last meeting with her son, Abdullah ibn az-Zubayr. At that encounter, she showed the depth of her intelligence, her resolve, and the tenacity of her faith.

Entrepreneurial Spirit

Her life is marked by her entrepreneurial spirit, resourcefulness in adversity, and ability to balance family and business effectively.

Involvement in Trade and Commerce

Hazrat Asma (RA) demonstrated keen business acumen and actively participated in trade and commerce. Her entrepreneurial spirit was evident in her involvement in various business ventures.

She managed her own wealth and engaged in trading activities, which was a significant achievement considering the societal norms of her time that often restricted women's economic independence. Hazrat Asma's (RA) engagement in trade was a means of supporting her family and contributing to the community's economic development. Her business dealings were characterised by honesty, integrity, and fairness, reflecting the Islamic principles of ethical commerce.

Hazrat Asma (RA) is celebrated for her remarkable resourcefulness, particularly during the early days of Islam when Muslims faced severe persecution and hardship. Moreover, Hazrat Asma (RA) managed her household efficiently while overseeing her business activities.

Her ability to balance these responsibilities showcases her exceptional organisational skills and time management. Her support for her family extended beyond her immediate household. After the death of her husband, she continued to manage her business affairs and provide for her children, demonstrating her resilience and capability as a single mother and entrepreneur.

Hazrat Asma bint Abu Bakr (RA) left a lasting legacy as a pioneering woman in trade and commerce, a resourceful and resilient supporter of Islam during its formative years, and a role model for balancing family and business responsibilities. Her life offers valuable lessons in courage, integrity, and the importance of contributing to society through both familial and entrepreneurial efforts. Hazrat Asma's (RA) story is a testament to the vital role women have played and continue to play in the growth and sustenance of the Islamic community.

Chapter Five

Zaynab Bint Jahsh: Leatherwork to Leadership

Early Life and Family Background

Hazrat Zainab (RA) bint Jahsh was the daughter of Umaima bint Abdil Mutalib, the Holy Prophet's (PBUH) paternal aunt. Jahsh (RA) bin Irbab, her father, was a famous immigrant in Makkah. She and her brother, Hazrat Abdullah (RA) bin Jahsh, were among the first to go to Medina.

One of the first groups of people to accompany the Prophet Muhammad north from Makkah to Medina in 622 was Zaynab bint Jahsh (RA) and her family. When Zaynab reached marriageable age, her family moved to Medina with her. Her Makkah youth flourished, and because of her exceptional beauty and nobility, she received numerous marriage proposals.

Numerous men were clamouring for her hand in marriage because of her reputation for beauty, knowledge, and wisdom. Her family belonged to the sabiqūn, a term used to describe the early generations of Muslims who persevered in following the path of Islam and were granted the good news of Jannah in Surah Waqiah. Her family was exceedingly well-off.

The Jahsh family was well-known to all the monarchs of the Arabian Peninsula, and they were so wealthy that her family held the keys to Baytullah (the Kabah). Nevertheless, the Jahsh family paid no attention to their wealth and status as the Islamic message spread throughout the city. Her siblings, Abu Ahmed bin Jahsh, Hamnah bin Jahsh, and Abdullah bin Jahsh, were significant companions of the Prophet (PBUH) and prominent Islamist pioneers.

Her Early Marriage

Zayd bin Harithah (RA) was a youthful servant who held great significance for the Prophet (PBUH). Following their arrival in Medina, the Prophet (PBUH) was looking for a suitable wife for Zayd (RA) and discovered that Zaynab (RA) had the traits he was looking for.

Many people had negative things to say about their marriage. Many servants found it unacceptable that a young woman of a noble family, who was also the Prophet's cousin, could do such a thing. It was a paradigm they had not seen since the arrival of Islam or during the Days of Ignorance (jahiliyah).

Prior to this proposal, Zaynab (RA) believed that the Prophet (PBUH) desired a marriage; upon realising that he was putting her forward for Zayd (RA), she declined. She did, however, agree to marry him when she realised that the Prophet (PBUH) wanted her to. Because of Zayd's genuine faith, the Prophet (PBUH) spoke to her about his own affection for him.

But she responded, "O Messenger of Allah, I cannot accept him because of the high position I hold in the Quraish." To this, the Prophet said, "I have accepted him

*to be your husband." Then a command from the heavens
was revealed on that occasion saying:*

*"It is not for a believing man or a believing woman,
when Allah and His Messenger have decided a matter,
that they should [thereafter] have any choice about their
affair. And whoever disobeys Allah and His Messenger
has certainly strayed into clear error." (Quran 33:36)*

Thus, Hazrat Zaynab (RA) obeyed the order along with the rest of her family. It was a marriage ordained by Heaven, as everyone knew. She gave it everything she had, but this marriage was simply not meant to be. As a result of their growing distance from one another, Hazrat Zayd (RA) went to the Holy Prophet (PBUH) to file for divorce. The Prophet (PBUH) advised him to fear God and not divorce his wife. (Sahih al-Bukhari)

Marriage to the Prophet Muhammad

Unfortunately, their discordant personalities and incompatibility made their marriage tense and only lasted a year. After Hazrat Zaynab's (RA) 'iddah (a brief period of time following a divorce or a husband's death during which a woman is prohibited from marrying) was finished, Allah revealed the ayah that is interpreted as follows:

*"And when you said to him (Zayd bin Harithah) on
whom Allah has bestowed grace and you have done
favour: 'Keep your wife to yourself, and fear Allah'. But
you hid in yourself that which Allah will make manifest;
you did fear the people, whereas Allah had a better right
that you should fear Him. So when Zaid had accom-
plished his desire from her (i.e. divorced her), we gave*

her to you in marriage so that there may be no difficulty to the believers in respect of (the marriage of) the wives of their adopted sons when the latter have no desire to keep them. And Allah's command must be fulfilled." (Quran 33:37)

Allah selected Hazrat Zaynab (RA) to be the Prophet's (PBUH) spouse, and He disclosed this to His Messenger. Although the Prophet (PBUH) dared not defy Allah's command, he could not inform anyone. He held this information close to his heart until Hazrat Zayd (RA) and Hazrat Zaynab (RA) eventually divorced. Talk of the father who wished to wed his son's ex-wife began to circulate, mainly since Hazrat Zayd (RA) was still known as Zayd bin Muhammad at the time.

The following are the words that the Holy Quran uses to address this:

"And you did conceal in your heart what Allah was going to bring to light, and you were afraid of the people, whereas Allah has better right that you should fear Him." (Quran 33:38)

But soon after, the Prophet (PBUH) received a revelation outlining a novel legal doctrine—namely, that an adopted son is different from a natural son. A man should only claim his own father's paternity. Thus, Zayd (RA) was renamed Zayd bin Harithah (RA), and Zaynab bint Jahsh (RA) was wedded to the Prophet (PBUH).

Moreover, about all this, Allah says as follows:

"There is no blame on the Prophet in that which Allah has made legal for him. That has been Allah's way with those who have passed away of (the Prophets of) old. And the Command of Allah is a decree determined.

Those who convey the Message of Allah and fear Him, and fear none save Allah. And Sufficient is Allah as a Reckoner." (Quran 33:38-39)

"Muhammed is not the father of any of your men, but he is the Messenger of Allah and the last of the Prophets. And Allah is ever All-Aware of everything." (Quran 33:40)

"Nor has he made your adopted sons your real sons. That is but your saying with your mouths. But Allah says the truth, and He guides to the (Right) Way. Call them (the adopted sons) by (the names of) their fathers that is more just with Allah." (Quran 33:4-5)

At the Prophet's (PBUH) and Zaynab's (RA) Valima (reception), which drew over 300 guests, ten individuals at a time would arrive at his home, remain for dinner, and engage in conversation. The Prophet (PBUH) was forced to flee his home and seek solace in the home of another wife. After that, the Ayat came to light, instructing the women to cover their faces when speaking with men in addition to telling the Prophet's (PBUH) visitors not to stay longer than they were invited.

Allah revealed to the Prophet (PBUH): "O you who have believed, do not enter the houses of the Prophet except when you are permitted for a meal, without awaiting its readiness. But when you are invited, then enter; and when you have eaten, disperse without seeking to remain for conversation. Indeed, that [behaviour] was troubling the Prophet, and he is shy of [dismissing] you.

But Allah is not shy of the truth. And when you ask [his wives] for something, ask them from behind a partition. That is purer for your hearts and their hearts. And it is not [conceivable or lawful] for you to harm the Messenger of Allah or to marry his wives after him, ever. Indeed, that would be in the sight of Allah an enormity." (Quran 33:53)

Before her marriage, Zaynab went by the name Barra, a name that denotes a very holy, pure, and upright woman. After their marriage, the Prophet (PBUH) renamed her Zaynab. It is common knowledge that a person's name might have some bearing on their personality. She changed her name from Barra to Zaynab to escape the conceit that would accompany the name. This emphasises how crucial humility is to Islam—it determines how close you are to Allah.

Because of this divine order, Hazrat Zaynab's (RA) life is now included in the Quran, which people can read day and night and use as a model for behaviour. For Hazrat Zaynab (RA), receiving such an honour was a source of pride. She once boastfully addressed the Prophet (PBUH), saying:

"O Messenger of Allah! I am not like the rest of your wives. All of them married you through their fathers, brothers, or even their relatives, but I married you by a heavenly decree from Allah." She often proudly claimed to her co-wives, "It was your families who gave you in marriage to your husband, but it was Allah who gave me in marriage to him from above the seven heavens." (Ibn Kathir)

The Prophet (PBUH) commanded that a lamb be offered to commemorate the marriage. The whole town spoke excitedly about the Prophet's first sheep offering, which was made during his wedding celebration. The entire populace of the mosque was invited to the Prophet's (PBUH) wedding feast, and everyone in Medina followed suit. With Allah's favour, there was enough food for everyone. Everyone appeared to enjoy themselves so much that they lingered until extremely late after eating.

Hazrat Zaynab (RA) spent the majority of her time in dedicated worship at the Prophet's (PBUH) home. She refrained from participating in the never-ending rivalry among her fellow spouses to gain the Prophet's affection. She was not jealous since she was sure of her attractiveness and faith. Hazrat Zaynab (RA) cared for the homeless and destitute during her free time in addition to her worship. She was an expert at piercing pearls and tanning skins; she marketed both skills and donated all her earnings to the underprivileged.

Purposeful and Deliberate

Hazrat Zaynab bint Jahsh (RA) had a slow decision-making process. She knew it was wise to consider any significant issue carefully and thoughtfully. She particularly held that one should seek direction from Allah before acting.

When the Prophet (PBUH) proposed marriage to her, many would have assumed that the answer would be an unequivocal yes. However, she remained neutral and prayed for guidance instead of making a decision.

"The Prophet (PBUH) sent her a proposal through Hazrat Zayd bin Harithah (RA). When he went to her, she was kneading dough; keeping his back turned to her, he gave her the Prophet's message that he wanted her to join the select group of the Mothers of the Believers. She said she could not answer immediately but would have to consult her Maker. She began praying to Allah for guidance." (Ibn Sa'd)

Without giving our decisions any thought, prayer, or fact-checking, we frequently make extremely public decisions. However, we might take a cue from Hazrat Zaynab (RA) and strive to imitate her thoughtful and calm demeanour, asking for advice and exercising patience.

Her Piety and Generosity

Hazrat Zaynab bint Jahsh (RA) was a member of the Quraishite royalty and came from a life of luxury. Still, she had a very tender heart for less fortunate people than her. Following the Muslims' victory over the Persians and their subsequent loot, Hazrat Zaynab bint Jahsh (RA) demonstrated genuine altruism.

"When Hazrat Umar (RA) sent Hazrat Zaynab bint Jahsh (RA) a portion of the treasure from the spoils of war, she instructed her maidservant to distribute it among the poor people of Medina. She named each recipient until all she knew had received a share. Afterward, she asked her maid to see what remained. Only eighty dinars were left from the substantial amount of gold, which she accepted gratefully as her portion, thanking Allah. Concerned that such wealth could be a temptation, she prayed to Allah never to witness such a large distribution of wealth again." (Sahih Muslim)

When Hazrat Zaynab (RA) passed away, the Medina poor were particularly grieving. This was because they were unsure of who would take care of them when a Mother of the Believers went through the agony of death.

She would philanthropically give alms and charity throughout Hazrat Umar's (RA) caliphate, to the extent that she donated her whole stipend—roughly 12,000 dirhams—that Hazrat Umar (RA) had put aside for the wives of the Prophet Muhammad (PBUH) during his rule.

Because Hazrat Zainab (RA) believed that accepting the annuity would be deemed sedition, she prayed to God to help her escape.

> *Hazrat Aisha (RA) reported to have said about her: "I have not seen a more pious lady than Zaynab bint Jahsh (RA). She was very righteous and truthful, she was very kind towards relatives, and she would give a great amount of charity and alms and worked tirelessly for goodness and to attain divine nearness." (Sahih Muslim)*

The Holy Prophet's (PBUH) wives would vie with one another to become more spiritually advanced and win their honourable husbands' affection. Normally, this would encourage some women to disparage the other, but the Prophet's wives (PBUH) did not act in this way. Hazrat Zainab (RA) was a deeply pious and devoted individual.

Hazrat Aisha (RA) once misplaced her necklace and had to stay behind in the convoy to find it. A companion of the Holy Prophet later accompanied her back. They did not say anything the whole way. However, hypocrites in Medina seized this opportunity to malign her, falsely accusing her of betraying the Holy Prophet (PBUH). When the Holy Prophet (PBUH) asked Hazrat Zainab (RA) what she thought about Hazrat Aisha (RA), she responded as follows:

> *"O Allah's Apostle! I refrain from claiming falsely that I have heard or seen anything. By Allah, I know nothing except good (about Aisha)." (Sahih Bukhari)*

Lessons to be Learned from Her Life

Hazrat Zainab bint Jahsh (RA) is a role model for all of us because of her devout devotion, kindness for the underprivileged, generosity, and attempts to support herself and others by working for what she had.

Initially, Hazrat Zainab (RA) opposed marrying Hazrat Zayd bin Harithah (RA). Still, she eventually accepted the marriage after the Prophet Muhammad (PBUH) persuaded her to do so and because she refused to disobey the 13th verse of Surah Hujurat. This tells us that the most crucial thing to keep in mind while choosing a spouse is that they should be someone who will guide us toward taqwa and possess the attributes mentioned in the Quran and Sunnah.

We can learn that women can engage in occupations not against their nature but in legitimate settings. Hazrat Zainab bint Jahsh (RA) traded leather that she tanned and polished, illustrating the legitimacy and acceptability of such activities for women in Islamic teachings.

Eliminating customs and habits that are deeply ingrained in a community and have nearly become religious in nature is extremely challenging. Extreme emotions are frequently triggered in society when widely accepted customs are violated. Because of this, Allah Ta'ala eliminated customs practised since the Age of Ignorance via the deeds of His Prophet (PBUH).

The Prophet's own cousin's marriage to a former slave disproves a custom from the Age of Ignorance that forbade a wealthy person from marrying a poor person or a noble person from marrying a slave. Though there is no distinction or superiority between people, it would be wise to emphasise one essential aspect: a couple preparing to get married should hold as close of a place in society as feasible.

This is referred to as kufu (balancing) in Islamic law. While not a pre-requisite for marriage, this equilibrium is now acknowledged as one of the tenets that facilitate peaceful continuation and long-term marital success. The fact that Hazrat Zainab bint Jahsh (RA) was selected to oversee and carry out such a significant legal matter and that she did not face punishment for it has greatly expanded the rights of women.

When Hazrat Zainab bint Jahsh (RA) felt that her ego was becoming too much for her, Allah Almighty prepared for her to marry Prophet Muhammad (PBUH) in heaven since she had followed Allah's and His Prophet's (PBUH) instructions. This demonstrates that even if challenging for us, we must follow Allah's and His Prophet's (PBUH) instructions to be blessed.

Furthermore, Hazrat Zainab bint Jahsh (RA) chose to be a mother to the impoverished rather than use her earnings for her gain. This is an excellent illustration of how working women need to spend their money. According to Prophet Muhammad (PBUH), the blessings of heaven shall be the reward for such deeds and sacrifices.

While Hazrat Zainab bint Jahsh (RA) was in a very challenging situation, she stood up for her despite their rivalry. She refused to let the occasional envy toward Hazrat Aisha (RA) control her. She taught us to control our emotions, especially when justice is served, and to stick to the truth when it comes to situations when individuals are being hurt by defamation or incitement.

Her Leatherwork Business

Islam is a complete way of life. Worship is when a Muslim does something with the intention of pleasing Allah (SWT). As a result, religion and business are not mutually exclusive. Islam has a distinct business culture with principles for conducting transactions derived from the Al-Quran and Hadith. Islam, therefore, has nothing against women who work, participate in the workforce, or help with business-related projects.

Hazrat Zainab bint Jahsh (RA) engaged in commercial endeavours as well. Zainab bint Jahsh (RA) was an exceptionally gifted and skilled woman, especially in the field of leatherworking. In her day, this trade was significant and well-respected. It entails the complex procedures of tanning and prepping animal hides to produce a variety of leather goods.

The Arabian Peninsula's population relied heavily on leather goods for everyday needs, which included shoes, purses, water bottles, and more. A keen awareness of materials and techniques was just as important to mastering this profession as technical proficiency.

Hazrat Zainab's (RA) proficiency with leatherworking was demonstrated by the excellence and robustness of the items she created. The intricate process of tanning, or preparing animal skins for leather, entails cleaning the hides, soaking them in a solution rich in tannins, drying them, and then stretching them to give them the proper flexibility and suppleness. This procedure could take several days or weeks to guarantee that the leather was durable and soft. Besides the tanning process, Hazrat Zainab (RA) was an expert in all phases of leather preparation and creation. She could support herself financially and create her own income by making and selling leather items rather than depending only on her husband or male relatives.

Furthermore, the success of Hazrat Zainab (RA) in the leather industry defied gender stereotypes and showed that women could be skilled workers who made significant contributions to the economy. Future generations of women will be encouraged to pursue their own entrepreneurial endeavours because of her commercial acumen and the high calibre of her products, which won her respect and acclaim.

Hazrat Zainab bint Jahsh (RA) was a great person in many ways, but her profound sense of giving and charity stands out. Her economic success served as a vehicle for supporting and uplifting people in her community and bringing her prosperity. Her strong devotion to philanthropy is demonstrated by the frequent utilisation of the proceeds from her leatherwork to support the underprivileged and needy.

Her altruistic endeavours frequently required her to make sacrifices. She is said to have given away a sizable amount of her personal fortune and profits to charities, demonstrating her deep empathy and sense of social duty. She gave because she was prepared to give up her comfort and luxury to help others, unlike some who might donate out of excess.

Her personal sacrifices served as evidence of her altruism and commitment to the community's well-being. She led a simple life, putting the needs of the weak and impoverished before her own. This degree of giving was a sincere demonstration of her understanding and compassion for others, not just a way to satisfy a religious duty.

Hazrat Zainab's (RA) altruistic efforts had an effect that went beyond giving people in need quick relief. Her example encouraged others to show compassion and charity, which spread goodwill across the neighbourhood. Her life exemplified how social responsibility and commercial success coexist and how riches, when used with compassion and a sense of purpose, could be a potent force for good.

Hazrat Zainab's (RA) life is a motivational illustration of how a strong dedication to social responsibility can coexist with entrepreneurial success. Her legacy serves as a potent reminder of the influence one person can have when they use their abilities and talents for the good of others. Hazrat Zainab bint Jahsh (RA) is revered as a model of kindness and charity who made a lasting impact on her community through her leatherwork business and unfailing generosity.

Chapter Six

Fatimah bint Muhammad: A Life of Devotion

The Beloved Daughter

Early Life and Upbringing

The most remarkable individual, unrivalled heroine, and unmatched herald in Islamic and beyond history is Hazrat Fatima Zahra (AS). When it comes to her father, she is unquestionably the ideal daughter; when it comes to her husband, she is the ideal wife; and when it comes to being a loving mother, she is the ideal role model.

Hazrat Muhammad (PBUH) and his first wife, Hazrat Khadijah (RA), had a daughter named Hazrat Fatima (RA). She was Hazrat Ali's (RA) spouse. She was born in Makkah roughly five years before Hazrat Muhammad (PBUH) became a prophet.

She inherited the best attributes from her parents from a young age. She was named Al-Zahra, which translates to "the fabulous one," largely due to her striking personality similarity to the Prophet (PBUH) of Allah.

Her early years were extremely challenging because it was at the time Hazrat Muhammad (PBUH) was bringing Islam to the people of Makkah, marking the beginning of his prophecy. A large number of unbelievers turned against and sought his death. At a very young age, she witnessed her father's hardships as he shared the gospel of Allah with the populace.

Following a few years of this anguish, she had to deal with the untimely deaths of her mother, Hazrat Khadijah (RA), and Abu Talib, who had been a fervent advocate and protector of her father. Following the death of her mother, Fatima took on the role of looking after her father, Hazrat Muhammad (PBUH).

Hazrat Fatima Zahra's Childhood

On Friday, the 20th of Jamadi-ul-Akhar, 615 AD, Hazrat Fatima was born in Makkah. Friends and Quraish ladies had counselled Hazrat Khadijah (mother of Hazrat Fatima) not to marry Hazrat Muhammad (PBUH). When she disregarded their advice, they were enraged and stopped visiting her. Hazrat Fatima invited them to assist her in giving birth when the time approached, but they all declined to attend.

During that period, Hazrat Khadijah (RA) received assistance from four stunning yet peculiar-looking women who identified themselves as Hawwa (the wife of Nabi Adam), Kulthum (the sister of Nabi Musa), Mariam (the mother of Nabi Isa), and Asia (the wife of the Pharaoh). They informed Hazrat Khadijah (RA) that Allah had sent them to assist her in giving birth. And so the child was born. After reading the "Kalimah," she entered the "Sajda."

Struggles of Hazrat Fatima (RA)

She was born into a difficult period in her parents' lives. Her father's opponents were all the Quraish Makkah residents who propagated Islam. Hazrat Fatima lived for around eighteen years, an age typically seen as childhood by the general public. However, this was not the case with her. We must carefully examine each phase of her life, as Allah chose it as an example for Islamic women of all ages and circumstances. Women in both their early and late years can profit from her exemplary life.

She grew up in a time of uncertainty and hardship. You will recall that the Quraish ladies declined to assist her mother in giving birth. She was saddened as a child to witness her father being harassed by Makkah's Quraish. As a two-year-old, she must have found it quite difficult to spend her days in Abu Talib's estate, where there was barely enough food for everyone. For three years, this was the case.

She was not even nine when her mother passed away. She continued to weep for her until Allah dispatched Angel Jibril (AS) to tell her that her mother, Khadijah (RA), had been granted a very prominent place in Paradise.

She developed confidence and patience from a young age a child. When no one else could assist her father, she did. According to Abdulla Ibne Masood, there was a time when the Prophet (PBUH) was prostrating (known as "Sajda"), and a Quraish person poured sheep dung on his back. He remained there until Hazrat Fatima (AS), who was not even nine years old, washed the dirt off his back. She served her father so dutifully that he called her "Umm Abiha" (The Mother of Her Father).

Every time her father was being beaten by the enemies of Islam, she would clean off the filth and dress his injuries. Seeing how distressed he was, she would cry.

But he would calm her, saying, "Don't cry, my little daughter. Allah will certainly protect your father and give him victory over the enemies of Islam." (Ibn Hisham)

Migration Period

Following the passing of Hazrat Khadijah (RA) and Abu Talib (RA), it became impossible for the Prophet (PBUH) to remain in Makkah. Allah told the Prophet (PBUH) to travel to Medina during the night. In secrecy, the Prophet (PBUH) travelled to Medina. It was entrusted to Imam Ali (AS) to bring the Prophet's family to Medina.

Even though Lady Fatima (AS) was in the house, she showed no signs of fear or worry; she spent the night in confidence and even though the tyrants caused difficulties when she travelled to Medina, she remained calm and trusted in God.

The path was treacherous. At a location known as Dhajnan, a group of eight Makkah ambushed her caravan. It was the Quraish of Makkah who had dispatched them and wanted them to return to Makkah. However, after Imam Ali (AS) engaged in combat with them, they fled. The Prophet (PBUH) was waiting for them at Quba, where the caravan continued. They then proceeded to Medina to begin a fresh life.

Umm Salma said: "After moving to Medina, the Messenger of Allah married me. He put Fatima (AS) in my care. I was supposed to educate her, but by Allah she was more educated and learned in all matters than I was." (Ibn Sa'd)

As before, Hazrat Fatima (AS) resided with her father. She was a carbon copy of him.

Hazrat Aisha (RA) says, "I have never seen any other person more similar to the Prophet's appearance, conduct, guidance and speech whether sitting or standing than Fatima." (Sunan Abi Dawud)

Bibi Fatima Zahra (AS) was a very lovely person who loved her father very much, which is why the beloved Prophet (PBUH) loved her so much.

The Prophet (PBUH) said, "Fatima is the sayyidat (leader) of the women of Paradise." (Sahih Bukhari)

As an adult, she developed into a stunning woman, combining the two extremely rare traits that her mother and father shared: piety and purity.

Zahra, or "the Radiant," was another name for Bibi Fatima (RA). Since these were the early days of Islam preaching in Makkah, Hazrat Fatima Zahra's (RA) childhood was the most trying period in Islamic history. Fatima has seen her father's suffering since she was a young child and always stood by his side.

Due to these extremely tense times she had experienced as a child and the tragic events that shaped her early life, Bibi Fatima Zahra (RA) spent the majority of her life ill. Despite this, she always showed courage and perseverance in adversity and supported her father (PBUH).

Relationship with the Prophet Muhammad

The bond between the Prophet (PBUH) and Fatimah (RA) is the greatest father-daughter relationship ever. When her father (PBUH) started spending extended periods of time alone in the highlands surrounding Makkah, Fatimah (RA) was born. However, their future relationship was not going to follow this pattern of remoteness.

Fatima (RA) was among the first few people to be privileged enough to accept the news that her father had become God's Messenger when she was just five years old.

When she was almost ten years old, the Prophet (PBUH) was praying in Masjid al-Haram when a group of pagan Quraish approached him. "The group approached the Prophet menacingly, and the leader, Abu Jahl, demanded, 'Who among you can bring the entrails of a slaughtered animal and throw it on Muhammad?'"

Among the worst of the group, Uqbah ibn Abi Muayt, offered his services and quickly left. While the Prophet (PBUH) was still prostrating, he returned with the repulsive dirt and placed it on his shoulders. May God bless him and grant him peace. The Prophet's friend Abdullah ibn Masud was present, but he was helpless to act or speak.

Fatimah observed this degrading act while her father was praying to Allah (SWT).Even at her young age, though, she refused to let it make her feel ashamed or even afraid. She washed the filth off her still-prayer father and railed at the offending parties, all the while maintaining her unwavering respect and love for him.

The heathen Quraish muttered nothing in answer, stunned at her outburst and audacity. While her father was being attacked, insulted, and hurt by the Quraish in Makkah, Fatimah persisted in standing up for him. As a result of her support, he felt more connected to her and her to him.

How many of us treat our fathers with this kind of respect as adults? Fatimah's tenacity and devotion teach us what it is to be a great and noble child. Being exceptional children to our parents does not require us to live under extraordinary circumstances. All it requires is respect and loyalty.

The Prophet's Fatherly Affection & Love

A common misperception is that a father's primary responsibility is to financially provide for his family rather than nurture them. He is often seen as the head of the household and the breadwinner. After all, raising the children is the mother's responsibility, right? Is it not a mother's role to instil in her daughters the values of being a girl and a woman?

Our community is negatively impacted by this misperception. Dads have a crucial responsibility in providing their daughters with care and nurture. To comprehend this, one need only look briefly at the Prophet Muhammad's (PBUH) bond with Hazrat Khadijah (RA), his fifth child. Hazrat Fatimah (RA) held a particular place in the heart of the Prophet (PBUH).

> *Aisha (RA) commented, "When the Prophet PBUH her approaching, he would welcome her, stand up and kiss her, take her by the hand and sit her down in the place where he was sitting." (Sunan Dawud)*

The Prophet (PBUH) treated his daughter with great dignity and respect, setting an example for her, the males in his immediate vicinity, and even us today on how to treat our daughters well.

Following the migration, the first significant event in the history of Islam took place during the Battle of Badr. During this time, Muslims were living in extreme poverty, and the Prophet (PBUH) had already been given the order to wage a holy war. Given the circumstances, it would have been reasonable for her to stop him from going to war as a daughter to show her love and affection. However, Hazrat Fatima (AS) consistently showed complete allegiance and selflessness and never showed any sentimentality against Allah's faith.

Proposals To Marry Fatima (AS)

Her father started receiving notes asking for her hand in marriage when she was barely nine. Two individuals who expressed their wish to marry Hazrat Fatima (AS) to the Prophet (PBUH) were Abu Bakr (AS) and Omar Bin Khattab (AS).

*The Prophet (PBUH) turned away from each of them,
saying, "Her matter is with Allah. Whenever He wishes,
she will marry." (Ibn Sa'd)*

The Prophet (PBUH) was then approached by Imam Ali (AS), who
requested Hazrat Fatima's hand in marriage. The Prophet (PBUH)
smiled, kept Imam Ali waiting, and walked to his daughter, saying, "You
know how near Ali is to us and how dear he is to Islam," according to
Umm Salma (RA), one of the Prophet's wives who was present.

"I have begged Allah to grant you a marriage to the most favoured
creature among His creations. What say you, Ali wants to get married
to you?"

Although Hazrat Fatima (AS) did not respond, the Prophet could tell
by looking at her face that she was pleased. "Allahu Akbar," declared
the Prophet (PBUH). Her silence indicated her approval.

Following the Battle of Badr, she wed Imam Ali (RA), the universe's
master. All the great people had wanted to marry her and had made
marriage proposals to her, but divine revelation turned them down,
stating that an effulgence can only be related to another effulgence. On
the 1st of Zilhajj and 2nd of A.H., their marriage was consummated.

*After the marriage ceremony, on reaching Ali's house,
the Prophet (PBUH) put Fatima's hand in Ali's hand and
said: 'May Allah bless His messenger's daughter. Ali!
This is Fatima, you are responsible for her. Ali! What
an excellent wife Fatima is. Fatima! What an excellent
husband Ali is. O Allah, Bless them, their lives, and
their children. Oh Allah, they are the most beloved to
me from amongst Your creatures, so love them too and
be their guardian. I put them and their progeny in your*

*protection from the evils of the devil.' He then ordered
all the women to leave the house." (Ibn Hisham)*

The words of Jabir bin Abdullah Ansari, a well-known companion of
the Prophet, are claimed to have provided a very fair summary of the
occasion of Hazrat Fatima's marriage:

*"We were present at Fatima's and Ali's (AS) wedding
ceremony, and indeed we have not seen any ceremony
better than that one." (Ansab al-Ashraf)*

A Life of Virtue and Wisdom

Fatimah's life was a living example of faith, endurance, and steadfast
adherence to Islamic values. She was the epitome of devoutness and
resilience because she remained faithful in the face of adversity. Her
elevated status and the depth of her faith are shown by her father's
announcement that she would be the leading lady of the women in
Paradise.

The Prophet Muhammad's (PBUH) cousin Hazrat Ali ibn Abi Talib,
whom she married, strengthened her standing in the Islamic narrative.
Together, they created a partnership that served as a model for moral
and spiritual instruction and was crucial to Islam's historical development.

Hazrat Fatima (AS) was an exceptional housekeeper and master. She
gave her maid and servant. Fizzah, permission to handle housework on
alternating days. Every other day, she and Fizzah alternated in doing
household chores. Thus, on a certain day, Hazrat Fatima (AS) would
take care of the home chores while her maid and servant, Fizzah,
rested.

This practice was developed during difficult times when the Prophet (PBUH) and Imam Ali (AS) were away from home fighting in different wars, and it is a testament to Hazrat Fatima's (AS) unwavering commitment to upholding human rights and human ideals.

Spiritually speaking, she was commended by Allah, prayed frequently, and refrained from worldly temptations. She prayed to God all night long for other people's well-being. She would prioritise the people in the Muslim community over her own relatives.

Hazrat Fatima (AS) was undoubtedly a wonderful mentor for her children. Her children's lives mirror all of her attributes: Hazrat Zainab (AS), Umme – Kulthum (AS), Imam Hassan (AS), and Imam Hussein (AS).

She raised them in a way that demonstrated advanced levels of intellectual, moral, and spiritual brainwashing. These individuals' lives and outstanding contributions during the darkest periods in Islamic history serve as evidence of the ideal upbringing their mother provided.

When Muslims settled in Medina, their economic situation gradually improved. Many Muslims gained wealth from the "Maale Ghanimah," or property and wealth acquired through fighting. However, Hazrat Fatima (AS) and her kin did not. They devoted everything they had to the cause of Islam.

The Prophet (PBUH) would often send travellers and others in need of assistance to Hazrat Fatima's home, where she would never leave them without something. She once gave a beggar her very precious necklace, which had been a gift from her cousin Fatima Bint Hamza, because she had nothing else to give.

In the final years of her life, her father left her the property of Fadak, an estate that reportedly generated at least 20,000 dinars annually, a substantial sum at the time. While she was free to spend this wealth, she only used what was necessary to provide food for her children. The remainder was donated to the underprivileged as charity.

Her Knowledge and Wisdom

Despite not attending school, she possessed a great deal of knowledge. She received her education directly from Allah and instruction from her father, Hazrat Muhammad (PBUH). The incidents listed below demonstrate the depth of her expertise. "What is the best thing for a woman?" the Prophet (PBUH) once asked everyone in the Medina Mosque. All responded, but none of them pleased the Prophet (PBUH).

To obtain Hazrat Fatima's (AS) response, Imam Ali (AS) went to her. "The best thing for a woman is to not see men and to not allow men to see them," the woman stated. The Prophet (PBUH) was happy and content when he heard her response. "She has obviously spoken the truth because she is a part of me," he remarked. She served as a teacher for ladies in need of daily instruction in matters religious and otherwise. According to Imam Hasan Askari (AS), a woman visited Hazrat Fatima (AS) with inquiries from her mother.

Hazrat Fatima (AS) patiently provided the answers posed by the mother. The mother persisted in her questioning. Hazrat Fatima (AS) was apologised to by her daughter. Hazrat Fatima (AS) responded, "Ask any questions that come up." "Would it be difficult for someone to be hired to carry a load to the top of a mountain for a reward of one thousand dinars?" she continued. Hazrat Fatima said, "My reward for answering each question is more (in value) than what it requires pearls to fill in the space between the earth and the sky," to the woman's negative response.

She recounted "Hadith" from her father, the Prophet (PBUH), on the prizes Allah would provide to Islamic scholars on the Day of Judgment. She is, in fact, among the most trustworthy sources of the Prophet's ("hadith") sayings (PBUH). When she appeared in Abu Bakr's court to request that he return the estate of Fadak to her, she delivered a speech (Khutba) demonstrating her comprehensive knowledge of every branch of Islam and every verse of the Quran.

This "Khutba" is lengthy, so we have not included it here. She cited almost twenty verses from the Quran to bolster her argument and demonstrate that Hazrat Abu Bakr was mistaken. Hazrat Abu Bakr was unable to respond to her. In her final remarks, she challenged him, saying, "So you do what you want and wait, and we too shall wait." Because of the superior quality of her knowledge, she could communicate with angels.

Allama Majlisi, who provides information based on Imam Sadiq's authority, informed her that she would be receiving some exclusive material that had been compiled into a book titled "Mushaf." This book included details on Islamic law, such as penalties.

The book also contained the names of all historical and contemporary world leaders and a description of every significant future occurrence. Note that this book was three times larger than the Quran. Recall that the Quran did not contain this book.

A Brave Woman

She powerfully portrayed a variety of characters during her brief life, and her societal achievements and outstanding efforts at raising her children have undoubtedly changed the course of history.

Her multifaceted nature is what allows her to manage all these roles, and her close relationship with God and her father, a prophet, is what makes such a performance possible. If Muslim women today want to be as brilliant and wonderful as Hazrat Fatima (AS), they will find great success both in their personal lives and in carrying out various tasks in Muslim society.

She was a brave woman who fought beside her father in thirty battles. Despite her personal needs and challenging circumstances, she supported the Muslim army, tending to the wounded soldiers, offering consolation to the families who had lost a loved one, and assisting the poor and orphans. With all her heart, she welcomed anybody looking for a solution to their problems.

Hazrat Fatima (RA) as a Role Model

Qualities of Hazrat Fatima (RA), who set a wonderful example for all women worldwide:

Hazrat Fatima (RA) is Infallible.

Infallibility, or loyalty, is the pinnacle of humanity. It is a fact that Hazrat Fatima (RA) was perfect. She was purged by Allah Almighty of all sins and imperfections and bestowed with every virtue, making her a role model for all women worldwide.

Lived a Simple Life Full of Virtues

Like her father, Prophet Muhammad (PBUH), Hazrat Fatima (RA) lived a simple life. She never entered this world; instead, she constantly treated others well so Allah (SWT), the Almighty, would be pleased with her.

Living in a two-room clay cottage, she (RA) dressed in the most basic clothes, ground wheat and barley, with her bare hands to make meals for her family and showed the highest kindness and love to her four children. Hazrat Fatima (RA) had virtuous morals. Hazrat Fatima's (RA) life abounds in spiritual activity.

Chastity and Veiling

For all Muslim women worldwide, Hazrat Fatima (RA) represents the ultimate model of chastity, honour, and veiling. Islam takes into account the preservation of women's morality and dignity to promote their sincerity and pleasure.

When we examine Hazrat Fatima's life (RA), we see that she has led a highly active social and personal life. Despite this, she was cautious in protecting her dignity and self-respect, and she never socialised with strangers. Hazrat Fatima (RA) stands as the best model for any woman aspiring to live a moral life in society, exemplified by her chastity and adherence to wearing a veil.

Altruism

Hazrat Fatima (RA) showed great compassion towards the underprivileged and destitute. Her generosity was evident from the moment she wore a new dress on her wedding day. Upon learning that a young woman from Ansar was without clothes, she donated her wedding dress to her.

Furthermore, Hazrat Fatima (RA) ground barley and wheat for her impoverished neighbours who were unable to do it themselves. She brought water to those who could not access it. Hazrat Fatima (RA) chose to live a life of selflessness and simplicity to please Allah Almighty.

The Ideal Matrimonial Bond

Hazrat Ali (RA) and Hazrat Fatima (RA) were wed, and following their marriage, she (RA) led a modest existence; her dowry was limited to items that met her most basic necessities. Previously, Hazrat Ali (RA) handled outside employment while she (RA) took care of her home and her two children, Hussain (RA) and Hassan (RA). Standing with her husband Ali (RA) and father Muhammad Prophet (PBUH) demonstrated her extraordinary bravery.

Confidence in Allah Almighty

Hazrat Fatima (RA) had unwavering confidence in Allah Almighty. Without a doubt, no one can question Hazrat Fatima's (RA) unparalleled faith and devotion. Her days and nights were devoted to worshipping Allah (SWT).

According to Imam Hassan (RA), he once witnessed his mother, Fatima Zahra (RA), performing Maghrib prayers and continuing to pray till dawn. Furthermore, according to him (RA), Fatima (RA) used to pray for every believer, man and woman, by name; she never prayed for herself. "Why do you not pray to Allah for yourself, Mother?" he (RA) questioned her (RA).

"O my son, the neighbour (first) and then the house," said Fatima (RA). Some of the admirable traits of Hazrat Fatima (RA) that we can use in our everyday lives and cultivate wonderful virtues are listed here. Every woman can achieve Jannah by imitating Hazrat Fatima (RA). For all women worldwide, Hazrat Fatima (RA) is the epitome of charity.

Bibi Fatima Zahra (RA) is a timeless role model created by the All-Powerful Allah to serve as a model for women of all ages. Through Fatima's own existence, the Almighty Allah enabled the Holy Prophet's (PBUH) faultless household to survive. The Islamic flag was to be passed from the Holy Prophet (PBUH) to Fatima's husband, Imam Ali (RA), and his offspring at their house.

The people who lived in Fatima's house were all members of the group of individuals chosen by God and superior to humans in all areas, including logic, science, piety, fairness, and righteousness. She is a wonderful example of patience, compassion, and morality for women of all ages. In all aspects of our lives, we ought to strive to emulate her way of living.

Hazrat Fatima's (RA) Demise

The Prophet (PBUH) passed away in the arms of Bibi Fatima (RA). She departed from this life ninety days following the Prophet Muhammad's demise due to an illness brought on by her intense grief. After the last rites were performed, she was carried into the darkness of Baqii Cemetery to be buried. Only a few family members attended the Prophet's daughter's burial (PBUH).

Her final day on this earth

On her final day on this earth, Hazrat Fatima (AS) was unwell in bed. At that time, Imam Ali (AS) thought that she had exhausted herself from cooking and cleaning for her two children, Imam Hasan (AS) and Imam Husain (AS).

Imam Ali (AS) questioned why she had worked so hard, and tears started falling from her eyes. She told him that she had seen her father in a dream the previous evening. She told him about the hardships she had faced after his death and how hard life had been without him. Her father, the Messenger of Allah (PBUH), reassured her that she would one day be with him, which gave her solace. It dawned on Hazrat Fatima (AS) that this was the last day of her dream. Before she died and was separated from her beloved children, she yearned to give them everything.

It was then that Hazrat Fatima (AS) gave him her last instructions. Her first request was that her husband and the people who had mistreated her not be permitted to attend her funeral. She wanted to be buried in the night's darkness so that this could happen.

Since Imam Hasan (AS) and Imam Husain (AS) would be devastated by their mother's passing, she asked Imam Ali (AS) to exercise additional caution with them. She suggested Imam Ali (AS) wed Hazrat Zainab's (RA) daughter Amana because she would raise the children well. Imam Ali (AS) was very saddened by this news, and tears filled his eyes. He (AS) bid her farewell and accompanied Imam Hasan (AS) and Imam Husain (AS) to the mosque.

Hazrat Asma Bint Umays and Hazrat Fatima (AS) were now left alone at home. To perform some particular prayers in remembrance of Allah, the Almighty, she asked Asma to leave her alone. After a while, she asked Asma to check on her to see if she was still living.

Hazrat Asma says, "I did as I was told. When I left her alone, Hazrat Fatima (AS) started addressing Allah and praying for the well-being of her followers. After some time, there was silence. I rushed to see what she was doing and saw that she was lying straight on her back. Her face was covered with a piece of cloth. When I removed the cloth from her face, I found her not breathing any more. She had left this world to join her father." (Ibn Sa'd)

As per her wishes, Imam Ali (AS) buried her in the darkness of the night. Besides Imam Ali (AS) and his two sons, very few others, such as Ammar, Salman, Miqdad and Abu Dhar, attended her funeral.

Hazrat Fatima (RA) bint Muhammad (PBUH) is an inspiration to all Muslim women. She was endowed with the finest moral attributes, most of which she had received from her father. These include courage, endurance, determination, and, above all, complete faith in the All-Powerful Allah. We should aspire to live like her in every area of our lives, not just daily ones.

Chapter Seven

Umm Sharik and Umm Ruman: Unsung Heroines

Steadfastness of Hazrat Umm Sharik (RA)

Umm Sharik (RA), the female companion of the Messenger of Allah (PBUH), was one of the fortunate ladies who persevered and remained faithful in the face of challenges along the path of Islam. She was a woman who was blessed with patience and perseverance.

This blessed woman, who did not give up surrendering to Allah Almighty and trusting in Him, enjoyed the mercy of Allah Almighty on multiple occasions. She did this despite her difficulties and continued to stick to her beliefs despite those difficulties.

This blessed woman, who did not give up bowing to Allah Almighty and trusting in Him, enjoyed the mercy of Allah Almighty on multiple occasions. Despite the difficulties she faced, she remained steadfast in her faith. Throughout the migration process, we notice the subsequent karamah.

Hazrat Umm Sharik (RA) found herself unable to locate a travel companion to accompany her to Medina. As a result, she embarked on the journey with a Jewish family. During the trip, she ran out of water.

Even though the Jewish household had an adequate supply of water, the Jewish man threatened that he would not provide Hazrat Umm Sharik (RA) with water unless she abandoned her religious beliefs. To intimidate his wife, he made the following statement: "I will destroy you if you give her any water."

The temperature was really high, and the sun's heat was intense. Travelling in those conditions without access to water made Hazrat Umm Sharik (RA) weaker. It was difficult for her to walk and speak. Because of this circumstance, the Jewish man felt a sense of hope. He had a feeling that she would soon abandon her religious beliefs.

Hazrat Umm Sharik (RA), on the other hand, experienced no doubt. Her conviction was so strong that she would never choose the hereafter over the world's existence. She had faith that Allah, the Most High, would assist her from some unseen source.

At a time when everyone else was sleeping, she had the sensation that water was being poured across her chest. She took the water and she drank it. To rouse the family, she yelled out. "I hear the voice of a person who has drunk water," the Jewish man responded. "I hear people who have been drinking water."

Astonishment engulfed him. As he shouted at his wife, he asked her the question. He was in a fit of rage. Hazrat Umm Sharik (RA) said his wife had not provided her with any water. The grace of Allah Almighty, she replied, was responsible for it. It was faith that the Jewish man had. In response to this karamah, he said the kalima ash-shahada and thus converted to Islam.

Hazrat Umm Sharik's (RA) unwavering commitment to her religion and refusal to renounce her religion resulted in a Jew abandoning his faith and converting to Islam. For this, she received the favour of Allah, the Most High.

Hazrat Umm Sharik (RA) provided the Prophet Muhammad (PBUH) with water and food whenever she had the opportunity to do so. The Prophet of Allah was more important to her than she was to herself. There was a time when she denied herself food to conserve a little butter for the Prophet (PBUH). Her maid was called and instructed to deliver it to the Prophet of Allah if she could. The maid carried out the instructions that were given to her.

The present that Hazrat Umm Sharik (RA) had brought was well received by the Messenger of Allah. "Do not tie the skin bag," he instructed the maid. Upon her return to the house, she hung it up in a location of her choosing. Hazrat Umm Sharik (RA) noticed the skin bag for the first time when she entered the house. It was so dripping with butter.

While on the phone with the maid, she reprimanded her by asking, "Did I not tell you to take this butter to the Prophet of Allah?" She was told by the maid that she had brought the skin bag to the Prophet of Allah and that she was unable to comprehend how the bag could contain butter.

All of them went together to meet with the Messenger of Allah. The Prophet (PBUH) stated that it was Allah's grace. The skin bag should not be tied, he instructed them. Umm Sharik (RA) went home with a smile on her face. This was the recompense for showing love and affection to the Prophet of Allah.

Her Marriage to the Prophet (PBUH)

Following this event, Umm Sharik (RA) went to the Prophet (PBUH) and presented herself to him as a potential spouse proposition. Although he accepted her offer, the Prophet (PBUH) did not go through with the marriage. Her death occurred in the fifty-first year of the Hijrah, and she never married after the Prophet (PBUH) left.

Impact & Legacy

Hazrat Umm Sharik (RA), whose full name is Ghaziyyah bint Jabir, was renowned for her unwavering dedication to spreading Islam. Despite facing severe persecution, she steadfastly continued inviting others to the faith. Her resilience was exemplified when she endured extreme hardships, such as being tied under the scorching sun without food or water. Yet, she remained steadfast in her beliefs, inspiring those around her. Hazrat Umm Sharik (RA) also actively supported Prophet Muhammad (PBUH), offering assistance and hospitality to Muslims in need, contributing significantly to the early Muslim community.

Hazrat Umm Sharik (RA) is remembered as a symbol of resilience and unwavering faith. Her story, marked by significant sacrifices and extreme hardships, highlights the struggles faced by early Muslims and is commemorated in Islamic history. Hazrat Umm Sharik (RA)'s perseverance and dedication in spreading Islam, despite facing severe persecution, serve as a profound inspiration, particularly for Muslim women, illustrating their integral role in the propagation of the faith.

Hazrat Umm Sharik's (RA) life exemplifies faith and resilience, teaching the importance of steadfastness in one's beliefs despite adversity. Her story offers modern Muslims a source of strength when facing difficulties. Her active participation in spreading Islam highlights the significance of being engaged in one's community and standing up for one's beliefs.

The Patience of Umm Ruman (RA)

Umm Ruman was the wife of Hazrat Abu Bakr Siddique (RA) and the mother of Hazrat Ayesha (RA). Thus, she was the Prophet's (PBUH) mother-in-law. Her real name was Zainab, but she came to be known by her family name.

Her son, Abdur-Rahman bin Abu Bakr Siddique, was an excellent horseman and master strategist in war. She taught him the meaning of valour and courage. She was a patient and tolerant lady who did not jump to hasty conclusions but gave matters deep thought.

This was evident in the way she handled the incident when people of loose tongues and small minds accused Hazrat Ayesha (RA) of adultery. When her husband explained to her the teachings of Islam, she did not linger with doubts about giving up the religion of her forefathers. She immediately understood the greatness of Islam and accepted it.

Abdullah bin Harith bin Sakhbarah Azdi, a young guy from her tribe, was the one she wed for the first time. By him, she gave birth to a son, and he was given the name Tufail bin Abdullah. She spent her childhood in a region of Arabia that is commonly referred to as Sarat.

After Abdullah bin Harith passed away, Umm Ruman (RA) and her son were left without any support. They then migrated to Makkah, and Abu Bakr Siddique married her after observing her vulnerability. This occurred not long after the death of Abdullah bin Harith. Before Abu Bakr Siddique converted to Islam, he was married to Qateelah bint Abdul-'Uzza.

Through this marriage, Abu Bakr (RA) already had a daughter named Asma and a son named Abdullah. Together, they had two children: Hazrat Abdur Rahman (RA) and Hazrat Aisha (RA), the mother of the believers.

In the very early days of Makkah, Umm Ruman (RA) converted to Islam. During the time that she was a witness to the awful atrocities that were committed by the Quraish against the Muslims, she would sorrow and cry for the innocent victims. However, Umm Rumana (RA) gained courage when she observed the moral strength and exemplary sacrifice her husband had made for the sake of Islam. He was a source of motivation for her, and having him around brought her a sense of calm.

The image of patience, endurance, courage, and bravery that Umm Ruman (RA) embodied throughout this extended period of time has remained the same. She devoted most of her time to praying and supplicating as fervently as possible to Allah.

As soon as she witnessed her husband's unwavering commitment to the spread of Islam, she immediately showed her respect for him and provided him with emotional support. The upbringing of her children in accordance with Islamic customs was the primary focus of her time and energy.

Hazrat Umm Ruman (RA) was glad to have such an honourable lineage when the Holy Prophet (PBUH) married Hazrat Aisha (RA). But as the years went by, Hazrat Aisha (RA) was wrongfully accused of adultery. Hazrat Umm Ruman (RA) decided to keep these rumours secret from her daughter. She merely humbly begged Allah (SWT) to reveal her daughter's (RA) innocence.

But when she heard of the rumour, Hazrat Aisha (RA) returned home and accused her mother of keeping it from her. Everything Hazrat Umm Ruman (RA) stated was, "O daughter, that is not important." According to Allah (SWT), gossip spreads more when a wife is regarded as lovely and well-liked by her husband. Hazrat Aisha (RA) was eventually shown to be innocent by Allah (SWT) in the Holy Quran, which is to be recited till the Last Day.

During this time, Hazrat Umm Ruman (RA) fell ill, and Hazrat Aisha (RA) took care of her till her passing (may Allah (SWT) have mercy on her). Going to her tomb, the Holy Prophet (PBUH) said, "O Allah, You know well what Umm Ruman (RA) suffered for the sake of you and your Messenger," pleading with Allah (SWT) to pardon her.

Impact & Legacy

Hazrat Umm Ruman (RA) was the mother of Aisha, one of the wives of Prophet Muhammad (PBUH) and a pivotal figure in Islamic history. Her diligent upbringing of Aisha greatly contributed to Aisha's later role as a key transmitter of hadith and Islamic teachings. Umm Ruman (RA) herself was among the early converts to Islam, embracing the faith alongside her husband, Abu Bakr, who was a close companion of the Prophet. Her supportive role extended to her family and the broader Muslim community, playing a crucial part in the foundational days of Islam.

Hazrat Umm Ruman's (RA) legacy is significantly intertwined with that of her daughter Aisha, whose contributions to Islamic jurisprudence, hadith, and history are invaluable. Umm Ruman's nurturing and support were crucial to Aisha's development into a key figure in Islamic scholarship. She is remembered for her piety, dedication to Islam, and her role as a supportive wife and mother. Umm Ruman's life exemplifies the virtues of faith, patience, and resilience, serving as a model of piety and dedication for the Muslim community.

Hazrat Umm Ruman (RA) underscores the importance of nurturing the next generation. Her role in raising Aisha, a key figure in Islamic scholarship, demonstrates the profound impact of upbringing and education. It emphasises the vital role of parental guidance and support in shaping capable and knowledgeable individuals. Additionally, her life illustrates the importance of support and solidarity, showcasing the value of assisting family and community members to foster mutual support.

In sum, both Hazrat Umm Sharik (RA) and Umm Ruman (RA) played pivotal roles in the early Muslim community through their faith, resilience, and support. Their legacies continue to inspire and provide valuable lessons for contemporary Muslims, emphasising the importance of steadfastness, active participation, nurturing future generations, and supporting one another.

Chapter Eight

Conclusion: Lessons from the Past

Importance of Female Entrepreneurs in Islam

Islam has pushed women into entrepreneurship to promote social and economic advancement. Nonetheless, they participate far less in global economic activities than males. Entrepreneurship has historically been perceived as a field dominated by men. Economic, ethical, social, and environmental aspects all contribute to the growth of entrepreneurship, and the application of Sharia principles catalyses this process.

Women entrepreneurs contribute to a nation's socioeconomic prosperity by reducing unemployment and poverty. The reasons women launch businesses vary depending on the culture and location. Women who participate in various business ventures can share the financial and social load of running the home with men in addition to receiving social and financial empowerment. Additionally, it will support their ability to make decisions on their own.

Islam has always granted women's emancipation and independence. Women-owned businesses are those that are founded and run by women. Women who exhibit intriguing personalities by actively participating in the socioeconomic support sectors of society are referred to as female entrepreneurs!

As demonstrated by the aforementioned instances, Islam has nothing against women who work, engage in the workforce, or contribute to business-related endeavours. Many of the Prophet Muhammad's (PBUH) female companions, known as Sahabiya, were involved in various commercial ventures sanctioned in Islam.

The Holy Quran and the Sunnah encourage men and women to work for legal income, meaning women can pursue business.

Inspiring Future Generations

Lessons for Modern Muslim Women

Countless examples of remarkable women throughout history shone as everlasting diamonds in their own right. Being the first to accept Islam, Hazrat Khadijah (RA) should make Muslim women proud. What about Hazrat Asma (RA), who was young when the Messenger of Allah regularly travelled to the cave of Thawr to find safety during his migration?

And what about the greatness of Hazrat Aisha (RA), one of the most prolific narrators of Prophetic Hadiths? As for Rufaidah Bint Sa'ad, she was one of the first Muslim professional nurses who could heal the ill and injured. It is stated that she participated in the wars of Badr, Uhud, Khandaq, and Khaibar.

What about the pride Muslim women can take in these examples? I could go on forever, but I want to refrain from asking you esoteric questions. I will discuss the ideal qualities of just three outstanding women who lived during the time of the Prophet in the following paragraphs. These women should serve as role models for all modern Muslim women and offer valuable lessons about life.

Hazrat Khadijah (RA)

Trading throughout the Silk Road, Hazrat Khadijah (RA) established a prosperous enterprise in a field dominated by males. She dispersed her riches so much during the siege of Abu Talib that she was left with nothing.

It is evident that Hazrat Khadijah (RA) was not only a successful businesswoman but also socially conscientious, with profit not serving as her primary motivation. She also gave the Prophet (PBUH) financial help.

Certain social institutions still exist today that hinder women's advancement and success in the corporate sphere. Still, Hazrat Khadijah (RA) is an ideal example of a woman who may motivate and empower women to develop their talent and spirit of entrepreneurship.

Her life serves as the best counterexample to those who mix religion and culture and do not support women pursuing higher education or careers.

Hazrat Nusaybah (RA)

Her most well-known performance was protecting the Prophet (PBUH) during the Battle of Uhud.

As soon as the fighting started, Hazrat Nusaybah (RA) provided water to thirsty soldiers and treated injured soldiers. But she quickly used her bow and arrow to create a human shield to shield the Prophet as the enemy threatened to take his life.

It is claimed that Hazrat Nusaybah (RA) would be fighting to defend the Prophet (PBUH) every time he turned in the Battle of Uhud.

Her legacy is a reminder that women are capable and on par with men and a mirror of strong Muslim women. We ought to keep in mind her tenacity and resolve and try to follow her lead in our own lives.

Hazrat Asiya (RA)

Hazrat Asiya (RA) endured Pharaoh's oppression but never gave up; her life, faith, and resiliency serve as an example to all of us. Although Pharaoh believed himself to be strong, tyranny is inherently weak. Despite being married to such a man, Hazrat Asiya (RA) refused to follow his ways, remaining gentle and kind.

Her independence powerfully illustrates how women are free to be whatever and whatever they want to be. To be truly pious is to have good character. Aware of the consequences, Hazrat Asiya (RA) refused to submit to Pharaoh's injustice in favour of a comfortable and privileged existence.

It can be simple at times to lead a comfortable existence and avoid dealing with the consequences that come from the actions of others. Hazrat Asiya (RA) shows us that courageous and bold women are possible. Being true to who you are empowers you greatly.

These are only three instances from Islam's history involving women. Looking at the biographies of women in this book can inspire Muslim women to live Islamic lives and spark their curiosity in the Quran and Hadith. Their legacy is one of bravery, moral rectitude, and unwavering adherence to the teachings of the Blessed Prophet (PBUH). For us to carry out our duties as sincere Muslims, I ask Allah to lead us as we strive to follow in the footsteps of these inspiring women.

Creating Balance is Mandatory

The urbanisation and modernisation processes significantly impacted women's position and status, causing women's roles to shift, which in turn caused them to start working outside the home. Working women's issues have long been the focus of discussion and controversy.

Women today have fewer responsibilities inside the home and no need to work outside of it than they did in the past. Many claimed that the rise in social issues in family institutions, such as disregarding certain privileges and responsibilities, which can negatively affect the family unit, results from working spouses.

Islam allows and even encourages women to work, granting them autonomy to decide whether to engage in employment. Nonetheless, women are not required to work if their expenses are covered by their husbands, fathers, brothers, or other caregivers. They are prohibited from working if doing so would be harmful to them. This principle is rooted in the tradition that women are entitled to support from their fathers or spouses, regardless of their wealth, to cover their living expenses.

Furthermore, it is unacceptable for them to work if their goal is to disregard their responsibilities as a wife or mother. However, under some circumstances, women might be permitted to engage in professions such as those relating to Fardh Kifayat, a legal duty that members of the Muslim community as a whole, including physicians, educators, and so forth, are required to fulfil.

To work, women must abide by certain rules, such as seeking their husbands' permission before leaving the house. Given women's nature, physical capabilities, and psychological preparedness, Islam forbids them from taking on physically demanding jobs that could endanger them or others.

Islam has made equality among men and women a reality in five key domains: shared human values, civic rights, education and employment rights, culpability and punishment. Islam does not distinguish between men and women with regard to public rights; the sole distinction is that certain obligations are specific to men because of life's necessities, the public interest, the family's interest, the interest of the woman, and each individual's personality. Islam views gender roles as complementing one another rather than just superficially depicting gender equality.

The primary causes of problems at home often stem from the hectic schedules and difficulties that working women face in juggling work and family responsibilities. Issues such as domestic violence, children's social issues, lack of affection, disobedience, adultery, and many more arise when a woman works. This is largely due to children's need for a mother's love and affection, which can be difficult to fulfil when mothers are balancing demanding work schedules.

Similarly, a wife's assistance is necessary for a husband to run the home. Furthermore, there is a correlation between the rise in divorce rates and the increase in female employment outside the home. Divorce can happen for a variety of reasons, one of which is that if a working wife discovers she can be a good provider, she may be more likely to choose divorce over continuing in an unhappy marriage.

To shed light on these issues and solve the social issues that arise in the family, we can turn to answers from Maqasid Syariah. It is crucial for families to implement quality religious instruction, particularly regarding aqidah and ibadah, to prevent family members from being involved in social issues. Keeping the family safe from immoral behaviour is critical for preserving the religion.

Second, in terms of safeguarding lineage, parents must ensure their children abstain from actions like adultery that would sever family ties. Love and care are, therefore, crucial to preventing this kind of thing from happening.

Thirdly, it is common knowledge that a working wife's role is to manage her wealth; yet, to avoid neglecting her family and divorce, she must adhere to the previously mentioned rules. Therefore, in light of Maqasid Shariah, this approach is deemed the best course of action.

When there is a conflict between defending religion and defending wealth, religion should take precedence. This is because protecting one's religion results in eternal fulfilment, which can be achieved by protecting one's money, soul, or mind.

The rise in societal problems is not solely down to the problem of working women. Many working women successfully run contented households, demonstrating that women can work as long as it conforms to religious guidelines.

To effectively govern their family institutions, women must have a solid understanding of their rights and responsibilities.

Continuing the Legacy

Islamic women entrepreneurs today stand on the shoulders of a rich and diverse history of female business leaders who were pivotal in the economic and social landscapes of their times. Modern-day Muslim businesswomen draw inspiration from these historical figures, preserving their heritage through various means.

They often integrate traditional values with contemporary business practices, ensuring their ventures reflect both their cultural heritage and modern innovation. By doing so, they help keep alive the stories and achievements of their predecessors, passing down valuable lessons in resilience, integrity, and leadership.

The Ongoing Impact of Early Muslim Businesswomen

The legacy of early Muslim businesswomen continues to influence and empower today's generation of female entrepreneurs in multiple ways:

Role Models and Mentors: Historical figures like Khadijah bint Khuwaylid serve as powerful role models, providing a template for success that blends faith and entrepreneurship. Their stories encourage contemporary Muslim women to pursue entrepreneurial ambitions without compromising their religious and ethical values.

Ethical Business Practices: Early Muslim businesswomen were known for their ethical dealings and charitable contributions. This legacy fosters a culture of trust and integrity in business practices among modern Muslim entrepreneurs. Today's businesswomen often emphasise corporate social responsibility, ensuring their businesses contribute positively to society.

Community and Network Building: Historically, Muslim businesswomen often worked within networks of trade and commerce that spanned vast regions. This tradition continues as modern entrepreneurs build and leverage networks within and beyond the Muslim community, facilitating mutual growth and support.

Educational Initiatives: The emphasis on education and knowledge, deeply rooted in Islamic tradition, inspires many Muslim businesswomen to invest in education and professional development. They not only seek to enhance their own skills but also to uplift other women through mentorship programs, scholarships, and training workshops.

Cultural Representation and Advocacy: By succeeding in various industries, contemporary Muslim women entrepreneurs help challenge stereotypes and misconceptions about Muslim women. They act as ambassadors of their culture and religion, promoting a more accurate and positive image on the global stage.

The ongoing impact of early Muslim businesswomen is profound and multifaceted. They provide a foundation upon which current and future generations of Islamic women entrepreneurs can build, ensuring that the values of faith, integrity, and excellence continue to guide and inspire the business world. Through their efforts, they not only honour the past but also pave the way for a more inclusive and dynamic future.

The life of Prophet Muhammad (PBUH) and the inspiring tales of many of his sahaba (companions) endured the test of time and inspired Muslims all around the world. The bravery, piety, wisdom, and power of the women who surrounded the Prophet Muhammad (PBUH), known as the sahabiyat, are still mirrored in the hearts and minds of young Muslim women today and will continue to be passed down to future generations.

The Prophet (PBUH), a man of the finest morals and character, was fortunate to have many sahaba (companions) who swore allegiance to him and supported him throughout his prophetic career. The Sahabahs were people from all walks of life, rich and poor, young and elderly, yet they were all bound by their devotion to and faith in Allah (SWT).

The women closest to and dearest to the Prophet (PBUH)—his wives, daughters, mother figures, and all those who battled for and aspired to be the most learned in Islam and its teachings—were likewise considered among the finest of sahaba.

This book honours these remarkable women by highlighting a select handful of the numerous inspirational sahabiyat, or female companions, who went above and beyond in assisting their community and were held in high regard by both men and women as role models for Muslims.

In the time of the Prophet (PBUH), Muslim women were fearless, brave, and driven to achieve their goals. They did not allow anything to stand in their way.

The rich history of businesswomen in early Islam provides a profound legacy that continues to inspire and shape the present and future generations of Islamic women entrepreneurs. These early pioneers demonstrated remarkable business acumen, ethical practices, and an unwavering commitment to their faith, laying a foundation upon which modern Muslim businesswomen continue to build.

Their stories highlight the importance of female entrepreneurs in Islam, showing that business success can coexist with adherence to religious and cultural values. After briefly reviewing the lives of these remarkable women, we can only hope that, as we move forward in our lives as Muslims and community members, we will retain the bravery, generosity, and spirit of the sahabiyat, the female companions of the Prophet (PBUH).

In essence, the legacy of early Muslim businesswomen is a testament to the enduring impact of female entrepreneurship in Islam. By continuing this legacy, modern Islamic women entrepreneurs are not only preserving their heritage but also paving the way for future generations to thrive and excel in the business world.

Find Out More

Website: www.barakahinbusiness.com

Socials: @barakahinbusiness

If you enjoyed this book, kindly leave a review to help expand our reach so others may benefit also.